tarot inspire

Marcus Katz & Tali Goodwin

KDP Edition

Published by Forge Press (2020)

1 Wood Cottage, Old Windebrowe, Keswick, Cumbria CA12 4NT

Find us in discussion with more than 35,000 Tarot Students, Readers and Teachers for the best in innovative Tarot in our Facebook group **Tarot Professionals** and enjoy the membership benefits of the Tarot Association at **www.tarotassociation.net**.

Tarosophy® is a registered trademark.

Cover: '2 of Swords', Tyldwick Tarot © by Neil Lovell

http://www.malpertuis.co.uk/tyldwick/

The world becomes an apparently infinite,

yet possibly finite, card game.

Image combinations,

permutations,

comprise the world game.

Jim Morrison, 'The Lords and the New Creatures', *Poems* (1969)

The Fool cannot demand or orchestrate this unfolding. It naturally fills the void of the Fool's empty heart, just as sunset follows night. He has to be fully immersed into the dark night of the soul, being prepared to relinquish all in order to empty the heart.

Russell Sturgess, *Metanoia: Renovating the House of Your Spirit* (p. 252)

INDEX

Introduction	6
Tarot Spirituality?	10
The Return of the Oracles	18
How You Work	26
How Your Universe Works	28
How to Find Your Spiritual Calling	36
The Circle of Oracles	45
Magick and Tarot	53
Mysticism and Tarot	57
Restoring a Spiritual Dignity to Tarot	62
A Map of the Spiritual Mountain	64
The Tarot Heliakos	85
The Tarot Shaman	100
Tarot in the New World	112
Conclusion	116
Bibliography	117
Websites & Resources	122

TAROT INSPIRE: A TAROSOPHY KICKSTART BOOK

A book to inspire your consideration of the spiritual dimensions of Tarot.

Introduction

In this third Kickstart book of Tarosophy teaching, we take a break from the reference work of *Tarot Flip*, the seventy-eight innovative Tarot methods in *Tarot Twist*, and offer a wider contemplation of Tarot – as a tool of spiritual inspiration. This is **not** a book about Tarot card reading in its sense of reading for yourself or others – although it may inspire new ways of considering that act. It is a short book of provocations, hints, and odd branches in the Tarot Tree – designed in a spirit of open wonder.

It is sometimes difficult for people to reconcile their use of Tarot in contemporary society, which has little place for such "superstitious" interest, so this book is given as an antidote to that negative outlook. We hope that it inspires you to explore the spiritual path denoted by this pack of cards and make new discoveries at every twist and turn.

This book is also a standalone title in the series, for those who are interested in opening channels to some of the philosophical and esoteric considerations of Tarot beyond the obvious mechanisms we have provided in our first two books. This may not be the book you are expecting, however it is meant to inspire your further discoveries beyond the matters dealt here – these are kickstart books of **your** creativity.

We have had a lot of challenges to bring you this book, which draws on material as old as the oracles and as new as today's latest tweet. We look forwards to continuing to accompany you on your own inspirational journey through Tarot.

Marcus Katz, The Tarosophist

& Tali Goodwin, TaliTarot

A Brief Note on IS and ARE

We usually try and avoid absolute statements. We think there is no "true secret of Tarot", no one "real meaning of the Devil card" or any such sentiments. We usually try and write in *e-prime*, a method of avoiding such absolute statements.

Whilst we may be lazy in this work, and not adhere to *e-prime* throughout, please take all forms of "X is Y" to be read as "in this particular case, X might be considered as holding some similarity to Y for your consideration". Or perhaps we are just writing for effect and marketing in some places, where the intent is obvious.

This is also why IMHO (In My Humble Opinion) appears online. No one thing can be seen as identical to something else, so when we say "The Moon is Red" we mean that in our language, to our perception, in a certain context, the object to which we refer looks like a particular color at this specific moment. We will take it as read from this point that we do not need to explain this in every sentence in this book.

Furthermore, in the interpretation of symbols, we can go by no better advice than Joseph Campbell:

> Since one's way of experiencing – and so, of interpreting – phenomenality cannot but be a function of one's own level or state of consciousness, there can be no one true way of evaluating life, symbolic forms or anything else.

> Joseph Campbell, *The Interpretation of Symbolic Forms.*

Tarot is the Book of your Secret

The Tarot is your blank bible and the book of your soul's secret. It has arisen - comparably recently in human development - over the last several hundred years and stabilized into a set of 78 images on material which can be arranged in a staggering variation of constructs.

We begin and end – and transcend both beginning and end – with the unnumbered or sometimes zero **Fool** card. As with all Tarot, the secret is not where it appears to be - the secret of this card is in the dog which faithfully accompanies the figure. As a symbol of true faith, a faith in reality, the dog constantly attacks the Fool at the same time as guiding him. He is the constant companion of experience – your experience of the World. His barking is not a distraction, it is direction.

And he holds an even deeper secret, woven into the very fabric of our experience of reality. The canine carries exactly 78 chromosomes. In life, these are the vectors of hereditary and are embodiments of two essential principles – **continuity** and **individuality**.

The tradition of Tarot is the secret of the Fool's Dog. These cards are a continuation of an evolving communication through **your** individual experience. Whether you simply read a deck, create a new deck, revert or recant the images, whether you follow one set of correspondences or another, whether you believe in angelic guides or the art of poetry to decipher the images, you are **continuing** an **individual** journey – through Tarot. And this is its tradition – a rose key (soul) to open the cross (experience) on which you are bound.

Tarot also shares this emergent property – it's most common number of cards (as ever, there are many variations) – with the atomic number of Platinum. This heavy metal has the properties of being resistant to corrosion and malleable to fashion into the finest of jewelry. Perhaps those attributes can be seen to correspond to Tarot in this contemporary *gematria*, or numerology? Perhaps our Tarot is the platinum level key to a spiritual world.

If we were to give shape then to the number, to find its vibration between pure number and illustrated image, the 78 becomes the 78 lines of Metatron's Cube, a geometric shape constructed from 13 circles and perhaps the most elegant arrangement of 78 lines possible.

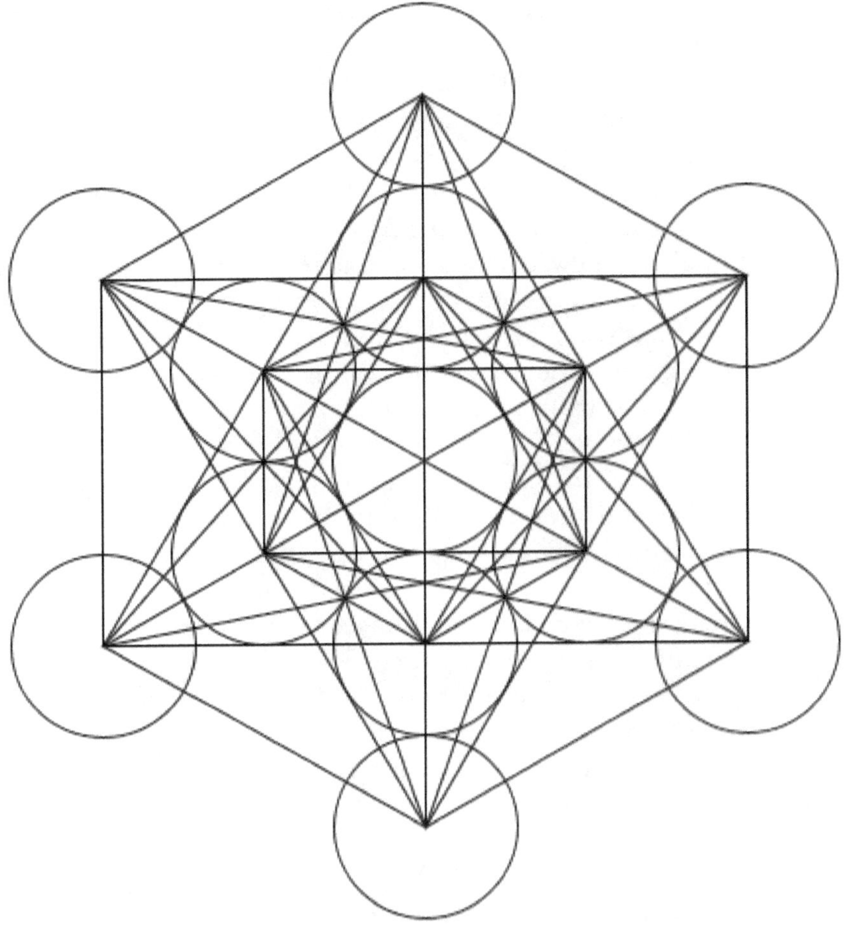

And of course, the 78rpm vinyl record. It appears that if you plug something into a hidden source of power, and try and give it shape and voice, the number 78 emerges naturally. In this context, the number is associated with that most nostalgic of personal items – a record of our own personal history, yet one common to all whom heard those songs. And so it is with Tarot – the same images, the same record – yet always, always, our own journey.

You are the Fool and your Reality is the Dog. Tarot is the song you sing to each other on your trip.

Are you the one who is living you now? This is the first radical question of the controversial spiritual teacher Da Free John (Franklin Jones, 1939 – 2008) in *The Four Fundamental Questions*. In this small book, he proposes four questions leading to a state of spiritual enlightenment, a state where:

> This realization thus becomes a radically new way of life, a completely new disposition relative to everything. You are no longer one observing and knowing. You are not other than what you appear to be. You are completely one with it. You are it. The release of the gesture of separation, of inwardness, makes the body whole. It becomes full. You are simply happy. You are simply the body. You are simply whatever is the case. You are removed from the game of conflict and discovery. You are at rest as whatever is the case. Thus, you see that you are radiant. You inhere and participate in everything and everyone. You are no longer separating yourself, no longer contracting, no longer entering into the hallucinated field of inwardness, but you are simply at rest in relations. In the midst of all this arising in which you have no independence, no view, no knowledge, you see that your radiance is perfect and infinite.

The Four Fundamental Questions, p. 37

This text, as many spiritual texts, finds its formulation also in our Tarot. As an enquiry into the relation of ourselves and the world, whether it be the Fool's or the Adept's journey (and they are sometimes one and the same) we produce descriptions of that journey both in text and in image. The Tarot is a montage of mystical experience – even in its most mundane presentations.

This is treated admirably by Evelyn Underhill in her seminal *Mysticism: A Study in the Nature and Development of Man's Spiritual Consciousness.* In her chapter on Mysticism and Symbolism – an absolutely essential read for anyone wishing to explore Tarot spirituality (in our humble opinions) – she writes about the various diagrams of the spiritual world. Whilst referring to symbolism ranging from Dante to Bunyon, to the Heavenly Jerusalem or the Seven Valleys of the Sufi 'Attar, she may as well be referring equally to Tarot:

> These special mystical diagrams, these symbolic and artistic descriptions of man's inward history – his secret adventures with God – are almost endless in their variety: since in each we have a picture of the country of the soul seen through a different temperament ... Thanks to the spatial imagery inseparable from human thinking and human expression, no direct description of spiritual experience is or can be possible to man. It must always be symbolic, allusive, oblique: always suggest, but never tell, the truth.

> *Mysticism*, p. 126

Her analysis of the three "cravings" depicted by such symbolism can also be of use to us in understanding Tarot spirituality; she speaks of the three cravings of the lost home, the heart and perfection. In this we see most deeply the narrative of Tarot in a spiritual manner – for the craving of the lost home leads to the Fool's Journey which is so often depicted in contemporary Tarot. The cards of the Fool, the Hermit, and in the Minors the Eight of Cups, speak of this pilgrimage. The craving of the heart for its perfect mate is seen not only in the images of the Tarot, but echoed in every question of the form, "When will Dwayne come back to me?"

And the craving of perfection, the "inward purity", this is seen in the various cards of devotion and religious or magical work, be it the Magician or the Hierophant, or the chapel of the Six of Swords. So perhaps we can wonder how the deck of seventy-eight images speaks to us of these spiritual longings; and look at each card afresh with three questions;

How does this image help me find my place?
How does this image open my heart?
How does this image bring clarity to my mind?

Furthermore we would recommend a number of books throughout this present work which may inspire your sense of spirituality in the western perspective. Here are several titles with which to begin that for us represent the pinnacle of spiritual experience:

- *The Path to No-Self*, Bernadette Roberts

- *The Love-Ananda Gita*, Da Free John

- *Daughter of Fire*, Irina Tweedie

There are so many more, of course. All books throughout are given in the bibliography or fully referenced within the text where possible. A useful anthology of western mysticism is *A Dazzling Darkness*, by Patrick Grant (London: Fount, 1985).

Is the Tarot a spiritual tool?

That cards have been utilized as a mechanism of spiritual, religious or ethical education is in no doubt. A pack of cards called the *Chartilidui Logicae* was published in 1507, being a "progressive instruction in the art of reasoning" (Hutton, 1979). There exists in the Victoria and Albert museum a deck of Christian Tarot cards. Kaplan gives examples of such decks demonstrating geography in a 1725 deck (Kaplan, 1985) and such decks as the early Minchiate of the late 17th century included cards expressing theological and cardinal virtues such as faith, hope and charity.

We understand that the esoteric architecture of Tarot was grafted onto the cards following de Gebelin's assertions, with the mysterious Comte de Mellet, of an ancient Egyptian origin. This was rapidly propagated in popular culture almost immediately by the marketing of Etteilla, in the late 1700's (see Dummet, *The Game of Tarot*, pp. 102-11). Following on from this offshoot of the original Tarot, the occultist Eliphas Levi then cemented the notion that Tarot was a repository of secret teaching – of which, he, of course, had been able "to understand the enigmas of every sphinx and penetrate all sanctuaries" (Levi, *Transcendental Magic*, p. 103).

It was then a rapid assimilation into the grand synthesis of the Golden Dawn (mainly through the Tarot work of S. L. MacGregor Mathers), and from there to Waite, Colman-Smith, Crowley, Harris, Paul Foster Case and all who followed.

From the 1960's to the present day, authors have touched upon the spiritual possibilities of the Tarot, notably in *Spiritual Tarot*, by Signe E. Echols, Robert Mueller and Sandra A. Thomson (1996). Here, for example, the Tarot Major cards are seen as a two groups of ten cards depicting the journey to spiritual wholeness; the first ten Major Arcana being "strengths and weaknesses", split into five "developmental tasks" and five "inner resources". The remaining ten cards provide "tests and dilemmas" on the journey to the wholeness symbolized by the World card. This is described as the successful outcome of the spiritual journey, representing "unity consciousness" (p. 101).

More recently, authors and teachers such as Rachel Pollack have provided spiritual contemplation through the deck, deeming it "an instrument of our wisdom because it contains the intricate details of creation, [but] also the method to use all that information" (Pollack, 2003). Dai Leon states that "used in the context of divination, the symbolic meanings, intuitive gestalts, and overall vision contained within each distinctive Triumph define the reading, guidance, and wisdom of a worldview founded upon ancient yet perennial knowledge and authentic spiritual realization" (*Origins of the Tarot*, p. 479).

So through the early teaching cards of virtue, the Christian iconography of early Tarot, the layering of esoteric teaching and its translation into new age thought and occultism, the Tarot itself has had a spiritual journey. Its spirit, if such it can be called, has reflected our own development – and continues to do so.

The Difficulty of Teaching Tarot

There is an elephant in the room when it comes to teaching Tarot or any other spiritual practice. This is not the methodology of training itself – although there are often good things to be said for teachers understanding the difference between training a "skill" and training a "method". It is the nature of teaching and education – and more particularly, its reception. We often have difficulties accepting hierarchy and teaching, particular where "fringe" areas are involved.

As an example, the concept of apprenticeship has almost vanished from western society outside of specialist trades and certain professions. The mastery of a skill in order to practice it professionally previously required an apprenticeship phase, a journeyman "proof by experience" phase, leading to a mastery that would be recognizable in and of itself. This guild structure – requiring a skilled master craftsman as its founder – has been largely thrown out as an obsolete hierarchy. We believe that there is still a lot to be said for learning ones skills from those who have mastered them through knowledge and experience.

In our educational system, we are taught from the outside in, and the modes of learning are constrained within propositional knowledge and logico-deductive reasoning. We rarely learn how to be creative, intuitive, nor the nature of belief, our place in the world, and the nature of awareness and our relationship to the Universe.

To find an authentic teacher requires that they be experienced in the journey. A wonderful demonstration of this journey and the role of the teacher (and the outcome) is to be found in the film, *The Silent Flute* (1978, also known as the *Circle of Iron*). This was co-written by martial artist Bruce Lee, drawing on Taoism, Zen and the teachings of Krishnamurti.

Our resistance to a teacher is profound, for we are taught a lack of trust in our own early educational experience. The gifted C.S. Nott, a student of G.I. Gurdjieff, whilst talking about how Gurdjieff's teachings would often provoke friction, also writes:

> In my childhood, and indeed later on in life, all sorts of persons, from my parents to my superior officers in the army, were constantly telling me what to think, feel and do.

Outwardly I accepted their views, inwardly I doubted them: I doubted whether they were speaking from inner conviction due to direct experience. Now I had met a man who, I was convinced, was speaking from his own experience when he pointed out my faults and weaknesses. By his own efforts he had overcome these things, and he fully understood my needs. The older pupils also, when they answered my questions about the system, spoke only from their own direct experience.

C. S. Nott, *Teachings of Gurdjieff*, p. 55

There is also a noticeable and recognized infantilism arising through the phenomena of social networks. Whilst certainly not decrying their usefulness in mass-connecting human communication, there are dangers inherent in the rapid rise of technology. In 2009, Lady Greenfield, professor of synaptic pharmacology at Lincoln College, Oxford, and director of the Royal Institution, made several stark warnings about social networking, suggesting that their overuse might lead to:

- short attention spans
- sensationalism
- inability to empathise
- a shaky sense of identity

She also pointed out that they are devoid of cohesive narrative and long-term significance, which might eventually produce adults with a marked inability to judge consequences of their actions and interact in real-time. We certainly hope this will prove not to be the case. It is also to be hoped that we continually learn and teach Tarot in a progressive and considered environment, particularly in a decade which has allowed any teaching to be carried out on a world-wide scale.

"It will rain," he remembered his father saying. "You won't be able to go to the Lighthouse."

The Lighthouse was then a silvery, misty-looking tower with a yellow eye, that opened suddenly, and softly in the evening. Now—

James looked at the Lighthouse. He could see the whitewashed rocks; the tower, stark and straight; he could see that it was barred with black and white; he could see windows in it; he could even see washing spread on the rocks to dry. So that was the Lighthouse, was it?

No, the other was also the Lighthouse. For nothing was simply one thing. The other Lighthouse was true too. It was sometimes hardly to be seen across the bay. In the evening one looked up and saw the eye opening and shutting and the light seemed to reach them in that airy sunny garden where they sat.

To The Lighthouse, Virginia Wolf, p. 152

In Tarot, every symbol is *multivalent*, that is to say, it can have a limitless range of meaning. A Sword can be the clarity of decision in one card and the pain of loss in another – in fact, on the same card, the same sword can be "letting go of the past" in one reading, and "making a single decision for your future" in another, dependent on its location. It is also affected by the context of the cards and multivalent symbols about it in a spread.

This is how Tarot works - as a simultaneous matrix reflecting consciousness – and Crowley himself said that the grasp of *multivalency* was the mark of the Adept. This is also why there can be no "one meaning" of any symbol or card.

When we talk about Tarot then, we are aware that we are only ever talking about one viewpoint, one lens, one here and now. **The Tarot is a transient, developing artifact of our relationship with the universe and ourselves** – as such, it is timeless and paradoxical. We offer here only one perspective, one beacon illuminating what it will, rather than any absolute house of light.

What is Tarot Really For?

Given the preceding notes that Tarot is whatever **you** make it, and in that freedom, we offer our own vision: Tarot is a mechanism of our relationship to the divine universe. Whether it is a reading for "When will Dwayne come back to me?" or the most mystical meditation on the correspondences of The Aeon card, these are both in essence, *enquiries*.

And the Universe is fundamentally an Act of Enquiry.

Tarot is a means of spiritual enquiry into ourselves, the Universe, and the relationship between these apparently separate elements. This is a spiritual journey. In making this enquiry through our Tarot readings and study, we test the Universe – and ourselves – increasingly exhausting (and making obsolete) – all that is not deeply true. Again, this is a spiritual journey.

One of my early teachers (writes Marcus) wondered why the first time someone performed a Tarot reading that worked, it didn't stop their world dead and send them on a journey to try and figure out how the universe worked to allow such a "non-apparent acausal" act to arise. There would be no need to do a Tarot reading ever again, he suggested, it would have accomplished its teaching.

As we progress, our internal sense of the Universe and our place in it, becomes increasingly more **comprehensive**, **consistent** and **congruent**. Tarot teaches us and we become expanded, connected and authentic. In that sense, we can be considered approaching values attributed to spirituality.

If Tarot is a language, then we must now take what we have learnt in that language to the country in which that language arose – it is only there so that we can communicate what we experience in that land, the inner landscape of our relationship with the universe itself.

The Return of the Oracles

Are you an Oracle or a Seer? Whilst there are many grades on the scale, in Ancient Oracular systems, the nature of an Oracle and a Seer were seen as polar ends of that scale. The Oracle, a word which comes from the Latin, 'Orare', to speak (L.) gave what the Greeks called *khrēsmoi*, oracular utterances. These were divinely inspired.

An Oracle was thus seen as a vessel through which a Divinity Speaks prophecy. This is also called inspiration. In Hinduism, it is the same as *Akashwani* , "a voice from the sky".

A Seer or *Mantis*, on the other hand, is trained and educated to use tools such as entrails or runes to offer auguries and does not need to be part of a "family" or "tradition" in order to carry out their work. Whilst we are no longer in ancient Greece, it is an interesting distinction in experience, as we each move between these two poles.

Sometimes a reading may be "by the book" and sometimes it may be utterly and completely divinely inspired – and sometimes, often, it may partake of the entire spectrum. The important thing is that we accept all approaches, they both have worthy forbears.

The Oracle Born in Blood

In *Tarosophy*, we concluded with a provocative challenge, a call back to the return of Tarot within the oracular tradition. We wrote:

> You speak with honey on your lips from the *Book of Clouds*, echoing the voice of fire from the living darkness, or you do not. There is no such thing as a half-way oracle.

In much the same way that the gristle and sinew of meat-preparation has been hidden behind the consumer-friendly packaging of a supermarket freezer section, so has the Tarot – and its near relatives, runic and stellar – been sanitized and slowly dismembered from its oracular roots.

As a system, it is indeed merely a few hundred years old, yet as an outlook, a perspective on the world; it belongs to a venerable wisdom tradition which was born in ancient blood. Amongst the earliest oracles were the Haruspices, who determined augers from the entrails and liver of sacrificed animals.

Illus. The Liver of Piacenza, 2nd-3rd century B.C.

The liver in particular was favored, for it is the largest gland available and rich with blood. It was seen at times as the centre of the passions, sometimes more so than the heart. The Roman poet Horace (65 BC – 8 BC) wrote "my liver fills with bile difficult to repress".

The giant Titysos, slain by Artemis and Apollo, had two vultures tear at his liver whilst he lay chained in Hades, and of course Prometheus, whose name may well mean "forethinker", was also consigned to a similar fate.

That the liver is remarkably able to self-heal has been arguably suggested was known to the ancient Greeks, whose words for liver and "mend" are very similar. So by reading the liver the seer is looking into the very physical world, the hidden inner world, the purely biological world.

It is from this root stock that the cardboard (paper, tree) of a Tarot deck, or even its plastic format (originally egg, blood, horn or rubber tree proteins), derives. We are a lot less messy; however we are still reading and interpreting the physical world in our hands.

That the light of Tarot can penetrate the whole body is of import to the very "feeling" of a Tarot reading. We readers know what it is like to have the hairs on our neck stand up during a reading, or other bodily responses to the oracular experience. We also know to recognize the flush response in a querent as the reading gains depth and penetrate to the very heart of the matter. A reading can be a visceral event, cutting to the quick or stopping breath, laying subtlety as a whisper or cleaning the edge of a wound.

As it is written, "the human spirit is the lamp of the Lord, searching every innermost part" (Prov 20:27).

The Wounded Healer

Tarot is a sum of many parts, in as much as Tarot can mean many special different things to so many people - there are many paths to walk in a vast world of beautiful choice.

There are many reasons that a person comes to know Tarot. It will help to differentiate between some of these choices. Some may have more professional considerations or more spiritual considerations - or both! It can be subjective and personal, it may be more mundane. There is the 'Tarot Reader' and the 'Reader of Tarot' or it may be the difference between 'Seer' 'and 'oracle'. There is the hybrid Tarot reader and reader of Tarot combined. However, one's approach to Tarot is as multivalent as the Tarot cards themselves.

There is a natural order/chaos at play, like attracts like and that is how it has always been and always will. This is something to be celebrated - *'vive le difference'*. If we were not, we would not be in the midst of the Tarot world. I, Tali, would not be writing this, if it was not the case. You may wonder how I see myself with regard to Tarot. What is my story? I naturally lean toward the intuitive side of Tarot, the occult; my intuitive side is the part that after a few diversions drew me to Tarot. A childhood spent of damping down my psychic nature as to appear 'regular' to fit in with the status quo eventually wore thin. I failed miserably of course; it is not something one can hide! Sensing too much can be a painful path to tread, and a lonely one. Your teenage peers are seeing boyfriends/girlfriends and you are seeing entities from beyond.

But you carry on and you work hard to be accepted and try to avoid revealing your difference. However, there is no way of avoiding where you are supposed to be, and where you are supposed to go. There is something called "answering the call", and this is related to the process of initiation and the 'Wounded healer'.

A large number of Tarot readers may have come to Tarot while they are, or have been in the past, seriously ill. The illness may have been one that triggered what is called a "spiritual emergency" or it could be that the experience of ill health has triggered a longing for a meaning which transcends an earthly one. Through the archetypal images of the Tarot we remember that what we once were, and that what we will be again. Is this what it is about illness that opens us up to the energies of the wounded healer in Tarot?

Perhaps it goes even deeper and we must take care of how we bring those wounds to our service as a reader. Guggenbuhl and Craig, a Swiss and an American, took Jung's references to the Myth of Asclepius, the wounded healer, and made a link to the complexities and possible complications that arise from counter-transference, the reaction that a Therapist can experience in response to their patients issues.

Metaphorically, this is the hot potato that may be passed back and forth between client/therapist, and if the "hot potato" is passed on to the therapist who has a psychological/emotional hang-up which has not been identified through analysis there could be a bit of an ouch moment, to say the least.

This is why Jung recognized the importance of analysts undergoing therapy themselves, and that the speed of the patients healing process is relative to the therapists own state. This was also described as "the therapist being just as responsible for the cleanliness of his hands as a surgeon would be before an operation" thereby avoiding cross-contamination.

Some people may be accused of taking Tarot too seriously; others may be accused of being too flippant. For example, some pole dance for a living and some pole dance for fun, some do it in public, some people have a pole at home and would never dream of doing it in public. Even in these whirly circles it creates a bit of friction between the different poles, how society views pole dancing, preconceived ideas of what it sometimes is and what it sometimes is not, but in the risk of mangling metaphors and being cliché, 'different courses for different horses'.

It all is as ever, as it is supposed to be. We can only ever be what we are, and not how others perceive us to be. Especially if you take into account that perception is so subjective and open to change at the drop of the hat.

It is all about us allowing that what is on the inside to be on the outside, and not give a flying fig! We are all on the path we should be on, just at times they inextricably meet and merge and then part again. We are alchemy at work, a spiritual work in progress.

> Who are we, who is each one of us, if not a combination of experiences, information, books we have read, things imagined? Each life is an encyclopedia, a library, an inventory of objects, a series of styles, and everything can be constantly shuffled and reordered in every way conceivable.
>
> Italo Calvino

We take our wounds, and we weave words from them. This is, in part, the power of Tarot — it allows us to expose our vulnerabilities, to heal in that process, and to re-connect our life-story in a way of ancient words.

The Way of Ancient Words

In our Tarot *Hekademia* 2-year Tarot course, one of the most popular modules deals with the oracular tradition. Whilst covering the basics of rune-craft, I-Ching and other divinatory systems, the most popular aspect of this module is that it covers oracular language. In this present kickstart book we would like to provide one such example for you to explore, based on Old English poetry.

It is provided as a different way of exploring journaling and "little white book" creation for your own Tarot, other than our Haiku methods given in other works. It is very powerful to explore a new Tarot deck as it requires good observation of the literal components and design elements on your cards, and then takes them into unexpected dimensions of oracular utterance.

The language structure we present here was common to poetry of Old English, Germanic, Norse & Anglo-Saxon languages. It is generally two half-lines verses (Distich) with a pause in the middle (Caesura). We won't concern ourselves with the two "stressed syllables" (Lifts) but just the alliteration which makes these poems so vibrant and forceful.

Alliteration is simply the use of the same sound/letter for two or more connected words, which gives them added emphasis:

See suddenly how swiftly she sighs.

Take time to travel without tension.

In this form of oracular poetry, we create our own Edda (like Beowulf and other classic old English texts) in what was called a *Hrynhenda*. We also take on this form by using only 8 syllables in each of the two lines of each verse. Those readers who have utilized our Tarot Haiku exercises will be delighted at the extra syllables!

Notice also how the verses are split in the middle. We do not generate a rambling flow of linked metaphors and poetic delights in this structure, nor the precise elegance of a Haiku. We rather take on a Klingon accent and guttural emphasis, and make pounding powerful poems of profound passion.

To create a Tarot Hrynhenda, and inspire your oracular insight, simply take one object that you can see on a card, and think of what it brings to mind – **whilst sticking to the same letter of the object**. Then choose something else, and do the same thing, whilst keeping the whole line of those two parts to 8 syllables.

Here we take the enigmatic 6 of Cups and see the flowers first, and the word that comes to mind, also beginning with "F" is "fall". Our eye then casts itself to the archway and the apex, so as those words both begin with the same letter, we write them down. This makes our first line of the verse, with a pause between. We put in the "and" to make sense of the line and reaching 8 syllables.

Flowers Fall | Archway and Apex

We then look again at the most obvious thing on the card, which is the children. Whilst we think about that, we also see something else that begins with "C", the cross. Whilst we do not have to have the second word actually something on the card, this works so we use it. All of a sudden, thinking about the falling flowers, the cross, the children, the man walking away, what arises is that this card is one of widowhood. The mother has died. We then see in the card that the "young girl" is actually a "woman", and the "big boy" is perhaps also a "man". Perhaps this indicates that the girl now has to take on the mother's role – we think this as we look at her "mittens", and as we do so, "Mother's mantle" comes to mind, making the last part of the second line and completing the verse.

Flowers Fall | Archway and Apex

Children and Cross | Mothers Mantle

In constraining ourselves to this old English form of epic poetry, we release our intuition – squeeze it into new outlets that could not be accessed in any other manner.

Here is a concluding example from a Tarot Edda journal, for the Hanged Man in the Haindl Deck – a deck *attuned* to this exercise and delivery style.

Ravens Recalling | Rainbow rite

The Hair of the Hill | Hugin Hail!

Hugin is the raven of "thought" and the hair of Odin All-Father creates the roots of the tree which is himself, "given unto himself".

In this reading of the card, the Hanged Man becomes a poetic stanza of self-sacrifice, memory and tradition. We see that the oracle has to give themselves to themselves and become the tradition. When we come to the Hermit, he is not *showing* the way, he has *become* the way.

In Tarot, we can reflect upon ourselves in any number of maps. We can compare and contrast Tarot to the levels of the Soul in Kabbalah, the aspects of the Self in *Psychosynthesis*, or the twelve parts of the soul as seen by Ancient Egyptians. The Tarot is a wonderful system of comparative illustration.

Here we will briefly explore how the Tarot illuminates our levels of being, from the most mundane to the most spiritual, through the eight circuits model of Timothy Leary. This has been brilliantly brought to life in the late Robert Anton Wilson's *Prometheus Rising* (1983). We would recommend this roller-coaster of a workbook to anyone interested in kicking open the doors of their perception.

This is also our section here on the Court Cards, as the Minors and Majors are treated elsewhere in this Kickstart book.

Leary proposes an 8-circuit model of the human make-up and our entire evolutionary course. These are, in summary:

I. The Oral Bio-Survival Circuit
II. The Anal-Emotional Territorial Circuit
III. The Time-Binding Semantic Circuit
IV. The Moral Socio-Sexual Circuit
V. The Holistic Neurosomantic Circuit
VI. The Collective Neurogenetic Circuit
VII. The Meta-Programming Circuit
VIII. The Non-Local Quantum Circuit

It is in the realm of the Socio-Sexual Circuit that Wilson takes Leary's model to apply to the Court Cards of the Tarot. He further presents a model by which these Court Cards correspond to the first four circuits – a model used by ourselves in the development of the Tarosophy Tarot.

Whilst admitting that Wilson perhaps bends the non-proven assertion to say "The clever Cabbalists who designed this pictorial key to the four primitive circuits included a clue to higher consciousness" (p. 114) we can certainly see a useful map.

Fire	Wands	Circuit IV
Water	Cups	Circuit II
Air	Swords	Circuit III
Earth	Pentacles	Circuit I

This mapping also corresponds across Jungian and Freudian thought, as well as the Kabbalah. It demonstrates how the levels of the psyche take on imprinting and we become our own "full deck of possibilities" having access to all sixteen types of Court Card. How those are developed in us depends on our natural biology, upbringing, and social conditioning – hence we become our own "card of the day".

To bring these elements into balance within ourselves, in order to escape from this "mechanism of delusion", Wilson suggests we work with the four extremes of the four circuits:

King of Wands	Circuit I	Oral Narcissist
Queen of Cups	Circuit II	Emotionalist Feeling
Knight of Swords	Circuit III	Rationalist
Page of Pentacles	Circuit IV	Sex Role

At these poles we see the four corners of our personal mandala. It is an interesting exercise to take these cards and contemplate our relationship to them, how they challenge us or seduce us from our own centre.

For further discoveries and delights, we heartily recommend Prometheus Rising, where you will discover that the Queen of Discs is "earth/water, a mixture of first and second circuit traits – sensational-viscerotonic-oral and emotional-egotistic-political. You better be dammed careful to call her Ms." (p. 112).

How Your Universe Works

The Universe, in its creation and evolution – and more precisely – our relationship to whatever that Universe is – has been mapped by many systems. From the obscure *Tertium Organum* of P. D. Ouspensky, the *Spectrum of Consciousness* of Ken Wilbur, or contemporary models such as *Spiral Dynamics* by Dona Edward Beck and Christopher C. Cowan. These systems denote different maps of the universe which can guide our own knowledge, understanding and wisdom, and the decisions that arise in us from these maps. Whilst it is often written that the map is not the territory, there are further rules to that in that the map can never be complete, and one can make a map of the map.

Here we will use Tarot to illustrate the spiritual map of the Kabbalah, embodied by the Tree of Life. This is to inspire you to consider using Tarot as illustrative of other such maps, from the *Bardo Thodol* of the Tibetans to the *Book of Coming Forth by Day* of the Ancient Egyptians. By extending your studies, this is no bad thing in itself, however to make comparisons of separate maps allows us to better triangulate our own position. It's like listening to two very wise friends, whilst still making up one's own position in wisdom within that triangle.

So in this section, we further illustrate the Tarosophy approach to Kabbalah, by taking the sacred Hebrew letters as illustrated – through correspondence of attributes – by the Tarot Major Trumps. In this way we can perform an illustrative numerology of letters and images, which we call a *Tarotria*, of the Tree of Life.

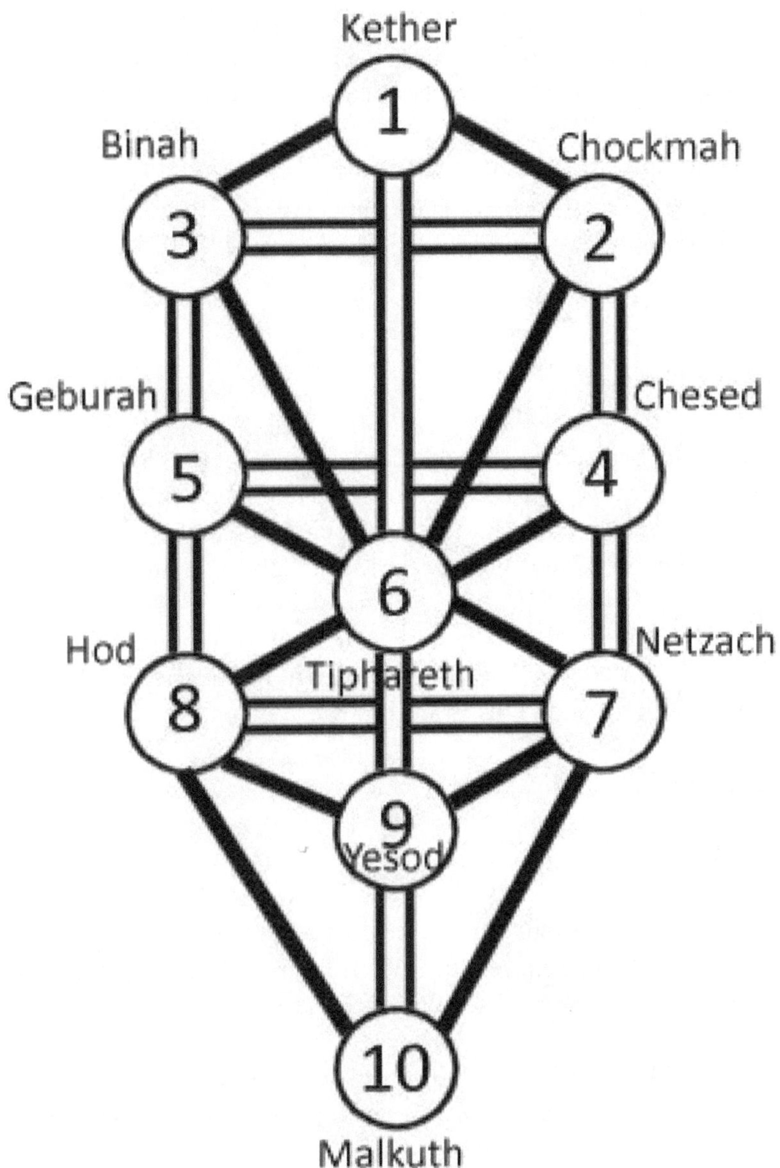

Kether
1
Binah
Chockmah
3
2
Geburah
Chesed
5
4
6
Hod
Netzach
Tiphareth
8
7
9
Yesod
10
Malkuth

We take each of the titles of the Sephiroth on the Tree and spell them in full in Hebrew (see also pp. 179-191 of *Tarosophy*) and then we illustrate these words through Tarot interpretation. In effect, this is a spread for the ten faces of the divine spirit in all creation.

You are encouraged to read our suggested interpretations and then carry out your own reading of the cards given for each Sephirah. We will then explore some practical usage of this mapping.

1. Kether, Crown: KThR

Wheel, World, Sun

On a cosmic scale, the World comes into being in Light and Motion. The great wheel of interconnectivity spins and throws out great arcs of energy and matter, coalescing the light into galaxies. The Wheel has no edge nor centre and the light is in all things.

On an individual scale, our centre, our root is a point of singular consciousness in a field of awareness. In its relationship to the World, it is enlightened. This is all that there is.

2. Chockmah, Wisdom: ChKMH

Chariot, Wheel, Hanged Man, Emperor

Gravity, strong and weak forces, begin to constrain the Wheel, the "first swirling", forces aggregate, and the dimensions are formulated up and down. Light becomes coherent.

On an individual scale, the sum of our experience of time, its friction and relationships, in awareness, generates a sense of being which is a mirror of all that is not-I.

3. Binah, Understanding: BYNH

Magician, Hermit, Death, Emperor

Now structuring, now containing the light, transformation occurs on a universal scale, devolving into patterns.

On an individual scale, awareness is channeled into a sense of selfness which can transform and be self-activating.

Da'ath, Knowledge: DA'aTh

Empress, Devil, World

This is the Big Bang, spilling the previous unmanifest patterns into manifest existence. Everything becomes attached to everything else. Things appear and disappear. Entropy.

On a personal level, we are born and begin to form attachments to our encounter with the universe due to the apparent separation of our identity. **This is the Fall**.

4. Chesed, Mercy: ChSD

Chariot, Temperance, Empress

And now the cosmic ripples expand, ever-increasing, something into nothing. All is in fusion and flux, nature becomes manifest, strings grow membranes grow quarks grow atoms grow molecules grow life. Everything lives.

Take those three cards, Google the Hubble "deep field" image, and ramp those up in your imagination together, the Chariot, Temperance (Art) and the Empress. Use the Thoth Deck. This will illustrate the nature of Chesed on the Tree of Life more than a thousand words.

In our personal world, these cards represent love. The paradoxes and duality of the Chariot, the merging and separating of the Temperance card, and the pregnancy of the Empress – all these together are the formulae of Love.

"For I am divided for love's sake, for the chance of union." (AL I:29).

5. Geburah, Strength: GBVRH

High Priestess, Magician, Hierophant, Sun, Emperor

This Sephirah on the Tree of Life is also called *Pachad*, meaning "Fear". It is used in respect of Proverbs 9:10, "fear of the Lord is the beginning of Wisdom" (i.e. Binah, the Sephirah directly above it – did you know many biblical quotes have direct Kabbalistic correspondence?).

So in a cosmic context, these cards represent the organization of matter and energy in various forms. The High Priestess may be taken by many readers as the embodiment of "intuition", however they conveniently miss the fact she is often depicted with the Torah – the law – in her lap.

We can only intuit something about which we know the laws already – a car mechanic cannot intuit which valve of your heart needs suture when it suddenly bursts, in a moment, whereas a surgeon can, based on nothing more than a hunch. A hunch, an intuition, which is an unconscious and rapid processing of a lifetime of knowledge and experience.

The Golden Dawn, incidentally, referred intuition to the Lovers card, connecting on the paths of the Tree of Life Binah and Tiphareth – understanding and awareness. They illustrated this with the rescue of Andromeda by Perseus from the Kraken. Just in case you were wondering how they got to use that particular image.

So the High Priestess here represents organization at a subtle level, the Magician represents organization at an elemental level, the Hierophant is the interface by which organization is transmitted, the Sun is organization through expansion, and the Emperor organization through focus. These are all in the nature of Geburah.

Personally, we experience Geburah, illustrated through these same cards, as intuition, channeling, revelation, awareness and will. The upper-level activities of our psyche prior to consciousness in the next step down, Tiphareth.

6. Tiphareth, Beauty: ThPhARTh

World, Blasted Tower, Fool, Sun, World

In the centre of the cosmic tree is Tiphareth, beauty and equilibrium. The Fool of Nothingness collides with the World of Everythingness. The World is actually dual here, to signify the meeting of our experience of reality and reality itself. The Blasted Tower is the connection between the world and the heavens, riven with the lightning flash of creation. There is no distinction here between the cosmic and the personal. All is together.

7. Netzach, Victory: NTzCh

Death, Star, Chariot

Netzach is below the veil of Paroketh - the veil is the noise or dust thrown up by the lower Sephiroth. It vanishes when they are brought into balance and stilled. It is the Sephirah of natural cycles, and given illustration by the combination of Death, transformation, the Star, now forming a materialized heaven in the night sky, and the Chariot, evolution taking its course.

In our personal experience, Netzach represents our emotional life, showing attachments and need/desire, hope, and emotional drive. It is a pure space of momentum and force, reaching out into the world. Many emotional issues can be explored in the framework of these three cards.

8. Hod, Glory: HVD

Emperor, Hierophant, Empress

In the realm of Hod, we have the lower reflection of Binah, formation. The Emperor and Empress sit on their respective thrones, breaking everything down into a simple binary division. Everything is male or female, positive or negative. The Hierophant passes these into manifestation as a bridge.

In our psyche, Hod is the mind. The cards illustrating the title show perfectly again the nature of the Sephirah. It is a space of digital distinction, either yes/no, pure logic, resulting in belief – the Hierophant. It contrasts sharply with the space of Netzach.

9. Yesod, Foundation: YSVD

Hermit, Temperance, Hierophant, Empress

At this penultimate stage of manifestation, now far from the original divine light, the foundation of material life is planted. The Hermit is the consciousness of life reflecting on the light, feeling removed and distant – the soul in exile. The Angel awaits us, in the enduring and abiding alchemy of the world, which calls us to awakening. The Hierophant and the Empress together embody the mystical process of *exemplarism*; Nature Teaching in its widest context. All that arises in the world is seen as demonstrating something of the divine – our only task is to read it.

To us this is the essence of Tarot spirituality; the use of Tarot to read the world until we can read the world in itself. We see through the pictures to the patterns, and through the patterns to the plan.

10. Malkuth, Kingdom: MLKVTh,

Hanged Man, Justice, Wheel, Hierophant, World

Finally, we have the sacrifice of spirit into matter, the world itself, the law of cause and effect, and the faith that we may return. And this is where the Wheel and the World turn full circle together – they are the two cards (letters) common to both Malkuth and Kether.

Here is a rare Kabbalistic insight illustrated and made obvious through Tarot; that Malkuth is in Kether, and Kether in Malkuth, but after another manner. The difference between them is the light is in Kether (Sun/Resh) and the Hanged Man, Justice and Hierophant are in Malkuth, showing us the paths to reconnect our spirit to the above are those of sacrifice, truth and revelation.

You will also see from a magical point of view that you now have the Tarot cards relevant to any creative act of magick. If you wish to bring about harmony, equilibrium and beauty in a situation, use the cards of *Tiphareth*; World, Blasted Tower, Fool, Sun, World in a ritual.

If you wish to gain deep *understanding*, place and contemplate the cards, Magician, Hermit, Death, Emperor, before sleep.

If you wish to discover how someone is attempting to gain *victory*, explore the cards; Death, Star, Chariot. To magically undo that victory, consider those same cards reversed and utilize them in ritual. In *Tarot Flip*, we give these cards the simple one-word keywords (reversed) as **Stagnation**, **Darkness** and **Stop**.

It is always incredible how this system holds together so strongly, as every map is based (underneath its geographical, temporal and cultural translation) on the same experience of reality.

The calling card of Tarot is the **Last Judgment**. It is the trumpet that awakens us from our deepest sleep. It is the calling of the spiritual life in the cemetery of material life. That calling is continuously brief; it is indeed always the "moment" of Last Judgment rather than an entire day. Here is how it is described in the alchemical *Cyhmical Wedding*:

> On an evening before Easter Day, I sat at a table, and having (as my custom was) in my humble prayer sufficiently conversed with my Creator, and considered many great mysteries (whereof the Father of Lights his Majesty had shown me not a few) and being now ready to prepare in my heart, together with my dear Paschal Lamb, a small, unleavened, undefiled cake; all of a sudden arose so horrible a tempest, that I imagined no other but that through its mighty force, the hill on which my little house was founded would fly into pieces.

> But inasmuch as this, and the like from the Devil (who had done me many a spite) was no new thing to me, I took courage, and persisted in my meditation, till somebody in an unusual manner touched me on the back; whereupon I was so hugely terrified, that I dared hardly look about me; yet I showed myself as cheerful as (in such occurrences) human frailty would permit.

> Now the same thing still twitching me several times by the coat, I looked back, and behold it was a fair and glorious lady, whose garments were all sky-colored, and curiously (like Heaven) bespangled with golden stars; in her right hand she bore a trumpet of beaten gold, on which a Name was engraved which I could well read but am as yet forbidden to reveal it. In her left hand she had a great bundle of letters of all languages, which she (as I afterwards understood) was to carry to all countries. She also had large and beautiful wings, full of eyes throughout, with which she could mount aloft, and fly swifter than any eagle.

I might perhaps have been able to take further notice of her, but because she stayed so little time with me, and terror and amazement still possessed me, I had to be content. For as soon as I turned about, she turned her letters over and over, and at length drew out a small one, which with great reverence she laid down upon the table, and without giving one word, departed from me.

> From the *Chymical Wedding*, 1984 Magnum Opus version edited by Adam McLean and Deidre Green, from the Foxcroft edition, 1690.

Every moment is a calling – and we are called by our future self to become more of whom we are to be. This is a fundamental reversal of the "I am made from my past" adage, and one taken up at great length by James Hilman and Michael Ventura in *We've Had a Hundred Years of Psychotherapy and the World's Getting Worse* (New York: Harper Collins, 1993). Here is how it can be seen, in the words of Ventura, who also refers to the Kabbalah prior to this quote:

> Development is no mystery, but the acorn is. Picasso said, 'I don't develop, I am.' *And the puzzle in therapy is not how did I get this way, but what does my angel want with me?"* (p. 70).

The whole notion that we are not ourselves, but we are whom-we-are-to be is also covered in *The Daemon: A Guide to your Extraordinary Secret Self* by Anthony Peake, and as experienced by Marcus Katz in *After the Angel: An Account of the Abramelin Operation* (Forge Press, 2001).

The blast of the trumpet reverberates throughout eternity, and our lives likewise are in a sense timeless. The Day of Judgment is ever-presenting, it is an "everlasting day". We walk in that moment effortlessly, and Tarot reading is another constant call to that remembrance.

When we journal a reading, we are making sense of a life lived backwards. We come to refer back to readings once the events they foreshadowed have occurred. We see new insight, new revelation. And this establishes sensitivity to our future calling. What is installed is what we predictive hindsight; the next reading we do has two voices – the voice we hear first as we look at the cards, and the voice we have been practicing, which tells us what they are likely to mean *after the event.*

It is this second voice from which we speak as an oracle. The voice that comes from the future place. We cultivate, orientate, gravitate towards this voice by constantly looking back over our readings, constantly comparing them. And eventually we do not require Tarot cards – we hear that voice in every moment and can only follow it.

The figures on the Waite-Smith image of this card make the signs of the Latin word LVX. However, this is only evident upside-down, from the Angel's point of view. The light of our calling shines upon us so brightly we close our eyes to it. It is only by turning backwards, seeing our ongoing past as a shadow of that light, that we can make our way in the spiritual quest. We walk backwards and eventually fall into the Divine.

Creating Your Own Spiritual Tarot Text

Journaling is a popular approach to learning and developing with Tarot. In this section, we would point you to Bobbi L. Parish's *Create Your Personal Sacred Text*, a practical and inspiring book. It provides a step-by-step guide to creating your own scripture, from your own experience of life, in your own words. This gives us a fantastic framework for working with our Tarot deck to generate our own sacred Tarot Text, divining our spiritual life.

We take for example here a brief method given by Parish to provoke writing when no inspiration can be found, a prompt for Tarot inspire! Parish suggests we ask ourselves to write, for example, about "sayings I have lived by". We give here our method of plugging this into Tarot:

1. Consider the question/prompt

2. Write about what it means, personally, to you, in your own experience and your own words.

3. Select a Tarot card which embodies for you the response to the prompt (or alternatively do this step before step 2 and select the card first before writing the response).

4. Then generalize out from your personal response and create a paragraph which summarizes the meaning of this card now to others, in the widest sense possible whilst remaining true to the card.

5. Condense this paragraph into a "spiritual truth" of the card.

6. Finally extend that spiritual truth into an "Interpretative Meaning" at a spiritual level for the card.

The following example is from Tali's Tarot Text:

Sayings that I have lived by.

My personal response: During my childhood I was bullied due to having Romany blood, I would be taunted either with the words "Gypsy, Gypsy Didakoi Gypsy" or be called "Kizzi" which was a book by Rumer Godden, about a half-Romany child Kizzi Lovell, who did not fit in with her peers.

I would run home to my mother who advised me to chant back at them, saying, "Sticks and Stones will hurt my bones but names will never harm me". I lived by that saying, I trotted off to school, the taunting starting all over again and I responded with my mother's advice… So did it work you may ask, did the children consider what I said, and think about their actions? No. So what was it all about?

Were they supposed to change their behavior? No, and you know now I look back and consider, that is fine, because the saying was for ME not them, I had to learn to harness a sort of "divine indifference". Would it have been better if I had punched them on the nose? No, I can only change my reaction, my behavior.

My card for this is the 8 of Swords. This shows how one can be blind to the solution that is always there for you and in this case when I was bound by my own denial of victimhood. It is also an interesting card because it shows the essential nature of bullying. I sometimes see this card as a woman who has been left by friends playing a game – and she thought it a game too. Now she has been left for it has turned into something else, but she does not realize this. This is often the nature of bullying from the victim's point of view, I feel.

Spiritual Truth: You are your own workshop.

[See also our description of this card in the Spiritual lessons of the minors]

The Interpretation of this card then in the light of the above, whilst you felt surrounded this is not a child's game, but something far more profound, it is something which you will return to time after time to remind you that you must take responsibility for yourself, stop cutting yourself off. The Swords that surround you can be your salvation and undo that what is binding you to the situation, or they can be picked up and your words used against you.

Other prompts given by Parish (pp. 160-1) also include:

- Patterns in my Life
- When I look in the Mirror
- A Place where I always feel close to Spirit

For reference, useful books on the nature of bullying, particularly in the workplace, which Marcus uses regularly in his NLP workshops, include:

The Sociopath Next Door, Martha Stout (New York: Broadway Books, 2005).

Dealing with People You Can't Stand, Dr. Rick Brinkman & Dr. Rick Kirschner (New York: McGraw-Hill, 2002).

In Sheep's Clothing: Understanding and Dealing with Manipulative People, George K. Simon, jr. (Little Rock: A.J. Christopher & Co, 1996).

How to Escape the Messiah Trap, Carmen Renee Berry (New York: Harper Collins, 1991).

Tarot and Inspiration

This idea of connection is of course very relevant in divination, literally, from the Latin, *divinare*, "to be inspired by a God". The breath can also be seen as an important part of divinatory practice, as the word inspire indicates – it literally means to "breath in" as well as inspiration being seen as "the authority to receive and communicate divine truth".

Many books make a great deal of intuition and Tarot readers often talk about the place of intuition versus non-intuition and so forth. I consider this somewhat misleading. Intuition is merely knowledge of something without the accompanying conscious knowledge of how that knowledge was derived. It cannot be done about something of which you have no knowledge! So a surgeon may intuit the right thing to do during heart surgery, without knowing how he came to a particular decision, but a shop assistant will not be able to do likewise – in surgery. Therefore, intuition is a skill that comes with practice, and knowledge – experiential or learnt. It can also be taught. Inspiration is a far more compelling concept and aim; to provide truly inspirational readings, with or without intuition - it doesn't matter.

What's Love Got to Do With It?

The divine love that binds the universe is depicted by a number of cards in the Tarot. In fact, we can say – like learning – love is a concept that is inherent in every image. We can see it in the Lovers, the 2 of Cups, the romantic gaze of the Page of Cups – love is everywhere in the Tarot. However, we got to consider this recent Valentine's Day how it was that the Major Arcana spoke of Love. We considered that love itself was always in relationship, the lover and the beloved – so we took our ears and listened to how each of the Majors loved their next neighbor. It formed a tunnel of love, a procession of hearts, and we saw too that this ring could be formed in a myriad number of ways throughout the whole deck.

In this, we take a trip as the Tarot tells in how many ways we love thee – in fact, 78 ways. Each card has a profound measure of love which can be discovered when they get together in the tunnel. We shall listen in as each card tells the next in what way its qualities reflect love.

And of course, this insight gives us useful information when reading relationship questions. In relationship, the cards themselves are transformed – the Emperor is actually here a card of "equality" not "dominance", the Empress is a radically transformative card when seen through the eyes of love … prepare for some surprises in the Tarot tunnel of love:

… so, why does the Fool love the Magician?

The Fool
I love you because you bring me back from the edge.
The Magician
I love you (says the Magician to the High Priestess) because I can never reveal the depths you conceal.
High Priestess
I love you (she says to the Empress) because you turn me inside out.
The Empress
I love you because you are my equal.
The Emperor
I love you (he says to him) because you can come out.
The Hierophant
I love you because you have what I can never admit to.
The Lovers
I love you (they say to it) because you can go beyond even love.
The Chariot
I love you (it says to them, both woman and lion alike) because you can pull apart.
Strength
I love you (the Lion roars) because you do not need another.
The Hermit
I love you because you have no responsibilities to others.
The Wheel
I love you, says the Wheel to Justice, because you align me to the journey.
Justice

I love you, because where I am blind, you see.
The Hanged Man
I love you, because you are my release.
Death
I love you, because you and I are the same.
Temperance
I love you, because you are not me.
The Devil
I love you, because you are all that I accomplish and fulfil me time and again.
The Blasted Tower
I love you because when I am gone, you are here.
The Star
I love you, says the Star to the Moon, because we share the sky in our difference.
The Moon
I love you, says Moon to Sun, because you give all that I can receive.
The Sun
I love you, because you complete what I began.
The Last Judgment
I love you, because you remain.
The World
I love you, she says to the Fool, because you recognize me.

You may wish to try this with your own decks – each has a surprising story to tell in the tunnel of love. As it is said, love gives us new eyes.

And for a Tarosophy "engage life" version: Take the Majors, go to your partner or do it for yourself. Each take a card. Look at each other. Read what it says from the list above.

The Circle of Oracles

If we allow the Tarot to talk to us, through a group of oracles, how does it tell us of its gift, and what does it tell us to remove from our lives – what blocks its voice? We carried out an online exercise with over forty Tarot readers and students to hear the voice of the Tarot.

Here is what we asked of people – and a method you can use yourself:

Take a deck. Shuffle whilst considering your role in life as an oracle - as a Tarot reader - as a priest or priestess - as a seer. Turn the deck face up and carefully go through the cards until you locate the High Priestess. The card above her is "on the bright pillar", the card below her is "on the dark pillar".

Now compose a piece of text as follows:

> "I am in the circle of oracles. On my bright pillar is [name of card] and on my dark pillar is [name of card]. I offer [interpretation of bright pillar card] as my gift, and remove from this place [interpretation of dark pillar card as a negative state]."

When we wove this spell on our Facebook group, here is what a circle of oracles sounds like together, speaking from pillar to pillar. Imagine our oracles dressed in the lushest of robes, in a misty and vast Doric temple … and hush, listen as they speak …

Marcus Katz: I am in the circle of oracles. on my bright pillar is the 2 of Wands and on my dark pillar is the 9 of Cups. I offer a vision of an elevated world as my gift, and remove from this place all self-satisfaction in that service.

Spike Andrews: I am in the circle of oracles. On my bright pillar is the four of Cups and on my dark pillar is the Chariot. I offer stability as my gift, and remove from this place all mental boundaries.

Nadine Roberts: I am in the circle of oracles. On my bright pillar is the King of Pentacles and on my dark pillar is the Knight of Swords. I offer the reassurance of generosity and reliability as my gift and remove from this place all insensitivity and intolerance of others.

Tali Goodwin: I am in the circle of oracles. On my bright pillar is the 7 of Wands and on my dark pillar is the King of Pentacles. I offer steadfastness in adversity by transforming incoming energies as my gift and remove from this place all control over dominions.

Michele L. Wolf: I am in the circle of oracles...On my bright pillar is the 10 of Swords and on my dark pillar is Strength. I offer light at the end of the tunnel and an end to struggle as my gift. I remove from this place the urge to control by force those around me and my surroundings.

Jac Alexis Ang: I am in the circle of oracles. On my bright pillar is the Queen of Swords and on my dark pillar is the Queen of Wands. I offer impartiality and clarity of mind as my gift, and remove from this place all self doubts

Fortune Elkins: I am in the circle of oracles. On my bright pillar is the Ace Batons and on my dark pillar is the Fool. I offer a secure career prospect as my gift and remove reckless speculation from this place.

Cally Palmer: I am in the circle of oracles. On my bright pillar is Ace of Wands and on my dark pillar is The Hanged Man. I offer an up surge and initiative for a new undertaking as my gift, and remove from this place and sacrifice things from my life to make way for this other new endeavor.

Lynne McGee: I am in the circle of oracles. On my bright pillar is the Ten of Pentacles and on my dark pillar is the Nine of Wands. I offer a strong united healthy future and full support for my family and I remove the exhaustion, anxiety and fears that these events may occur again.

Carina Arveklev: I am in the circle of oracles, on my bright pillar is the Tower and on my dark pillar is Two of Swords. I offer ability to stay calm when all seems to crumble and fall around you as my gift and I remove all feelings and thoughts that are not your own.

Tara O'Brien: I am in the circle of oracles. On my bright pillar is the Ten of Cups and on my dark pillar is the Fool. I offer the joy that comes from living/realizing your dreams through love and service and I remove from this place naivety and foolhardy gullibility.

Steph Myriel Es-Tragon: I am in the circle of oracles. On my bright pillar is the 2 of Pentacles and on my dark pillar is the Blasted Tower. I offer the joy in sharing resources and creative work as my gift and remove from this place the fear regarding rapid unexpected change.

Kareena Narwani: I am in the circle of oracles. On my bright pillar is the Empress and on my dark pillar is the 5 of Pentacles. I offer creativity, fertility and love as my gift and I remove from this place loneliness and sorrow.

Janine Worthington: I am in the circle of oracles on my bright side is the king of cups and on my dark side is the death card...I offer impartial emotional guidance and a shoulder to cry on and remove from this place the fear to follow your path and change one's life for the better

Camelia Elias: I am in the circle of oracles. On my bright pillar is the Roy de Couppes and on my dark pillar is Le Bateleur. I offer responsible love as my gift and remove the seducer from this place.

Catherine Chandler: I am in the circle of oracles. On my bright pillar is the 4 of Pentacles and on my dark pillar is the 7 of wands. I offer a vision of fruitful harvest from your own endeavor, guided by a greater source and remove from this place the possible overbearing insistence of a different force wishing to join with you that could shake your foundations.

Richard Abbot: I am in the circle of oracles. On my bright pillar is Justice (XI) and on my dark pillar is The Magician (I). I offer an understanding of cause and effect and a balanced perspective as my gift, and remove from this place narrow personal desires and notions of instant gratification.

Claire Galvin: I am in the circle of Oracles. On my bright pillar is the Queen of Wands and on my dark pillar is the Magician. I offer creative vision, true friendship and remove from this place conceitedness and self sabotage.

Jeffrey M. Donato: I am in the circle of oracles. On my bright pillar is Strength and on my dark pillar is the Knight of Wands. I offer the virtue of fortitude, and a patient willingness to work towards deciphering meaning for others as my gift, and remove from this place all expectation and destructive impulse. I tear down the subconscious barriers and help others to recognize their true natures.

Cheryl Savino: I am in the circle of oracles. on my bright pillar is the King of Swords and on my dark pillar is The Hermit. I offer just and ethical insights as my gift, and remove from this place seclusion and introspection in that service.

Sissi Fraley: I am in the circle of Oracles. On my bright pillar is the 5 of Swords (rev) and on my dark pillar is the King of Swords (rev). I offer forgiveness and change and remove from this place anger, bitterness, and resentment.

Shay Lefebvre: I am in the circle of Oracles. On my bright pillar is the Seven of Pentacles and on my dark pillar is the Three of Wands. I offer appreciation of what you have before you and remove speculation that the grass may be greener elsewhere.

TarotCard-reader Mohini: I am in the circle of Oracles. On my bright pillar is Two of Cups and on my dark pillar is The Tower. I offer the vision of highest love and partnering with divinity.... and remove from this place the need to have any facade to protect the truth.

Susa Morgan Black: I am in the circle of oracles. On my bright pillar is the 5 of Pentacles and on my dark pillar is the Page of Wands reversed. I offer a vision of sanctuary for the wounded as my gift, and remove from this place all aimless wandering in search of sanctuary.

James Wells: I am in the circle of oracles. On my bright pillar is the Tower and on my dark pillar is the Five of Pentacles. I offer an unwavering voice of thunder as my gift, and remove from this place all that is injurious and penurious.

Pauline Devlin: I am in the circle of oracles, on my bright pillar is the 3 of swords and on my dark pillar is the lovers. I offer a vision of discernment in relationships, of accepting the teachings and loss from within them, and remove from this place all choices that I truly know are irresponsible and will love myself as much as I love another.

Katie-Ellen Hazeldine: I am in the circle of oracles. On my bright pillar is The Chariot. On my dark pillar is the 8 of Swords. I offer mirrors and words for harmonization and congruency, supporting peace of clarity within, enabling progress of thought and action without. I serve to remove bars from cages that needlessly oppress and confine, that are prisons not sanctuaries. I help the difference to be known, in order that there shall be liberation from confusion, which blinds and shackles.

Barbara Moore: I am in the circle of oracles. On my bright pillar is Death. On my dark pillar is Strength. I offer guidance through the darkest hours of transformation and remove from this place the need the need to be a savior.

Prema Lawrence: I am in the circle of oracles. On my bright pillar is the Fool. On my dark pillar is Judgment. I offer the rites of passage and the path to the journey and new beginnings with absolute child-like innocence and remove any rules and regulations that will hold the butterflies from coming out of their pupas. I let go of any stereotype perceptions that may hold back people from finding themselves. I embrace the uniqueness of each one's purpose.

Janine Hall: I am in the circle of oracles. On my bright pillar is the Four of Wands and on my dark pillar is Six of Swords. I offer celebration and my confidence in your truths, passions and ambitions as my gift, and remove from this place the storminess caused by upset minds.

Sarah Schuster: I am in the Circle of Oracles. On my bright pillar is the Magician and on my dark pillar is the Dancer Prince. I offer potential in communication as well as in intelligence and the tools for inner strength, power and understanding as my Gift and remove from this place obsessiveness and all senses of been stifled by undesired emotions.

Emma Morley: I am in the Circle of Oracles. On my bright pillar is Temperance and on my dark pillar is the 2 of Wands. I offer guidance with calm, centered deliberation, delivering tactful and sympathetic advice without sugar-coating as my gift, and I remove from this place old fashioned, stunted views and feelings of self-doubt.

Den Elder: I am in the circle of oracles. On my bright pillar is 4 Rods and on my dark pillar is 7 Cups. I offer a happy partnership as my gift, and remove from this place the waste of time of wishful thinking without action.

Carole McCleery: I am in the circle of oracles. On my bright pillar is the Hierophant on my dark pillar is the 10 of Wands. I offer counselling and spiritual support as my gift and remove the burdens of your life in that service.

Ivy Lieberman: I am in the circle of oracles. On my bright pillar is 7 of cups and on my dark pillar is 9 of swords. I offer vision and clarity as my gift, and remove from this place the madness of false hope in dreams.

Kim Cadotte: I am in the Circle of Oracles. On my bright pillar is Elder of Earth and on my dark pillar is the Three of Air. I offer a lifestyle of simplicity and self sufficiency as my gift, and I remove from this place old patterns and the tendency to over think things.

Stacey Riley: I am in the Circle of Oracles. On my bright Pillar is the 10 of Cups and on my dark pillar is the six of coins. I offer my imagination at its fullest potential as my gift and remove from this place my want for more than I have.

Krsna-Nandini Main: I am in the circle of oracles. On my bright pillar is the 8 of swords and on my dark pillar is the 3 of swords. I offer the ability to show you your restrictions as my gift and I remove from this place the heartache associated with feelings of unworthiness and lack of belief in myself.

Alan John Wilkinson: I am in the circle of oracles. On my bright pillar is the 10 of Swords and on my dark pillar is the 6 of cups. I offer hope when there appears to be none, and remove from this place stuck memories from the past.

Lori Grace Petroff: I am in the Circle of Oracles. On my Bright pillar is The High Priest. On my dark pillar is the Nine of Pentacles. I offer an earthbound magic, bring respect and clarity to the very real and touchable side of magic, as my gift. I remove from this place the ego, the need to hoard and hide away skills and gifts, and the traps of money.

Sarah Perks: I am in the circle of oracles. On my bright pillar is the King of Cups and on my dark pillar is the 7 of Swords. I offer kindness, compassion and support without judgment; I try to facilitate harmony through my actions, as my gift. I remove from this place, self deception.

Marcia McCord: I am in the circle of oracles. On my bright pillar is the Ace of Swords and on my dark pillar is the 9 of Pentacles. I offer new ideas and perspectives as my gift, and remove from this place the limitations of the Comfort Zone and complacency.

Sherry Warner: I am in the circle of oracles. On my bright pillar is Wheel of Fortune (rev) and on my dark pillar is Knight of Cups (rev). I offer insight into the ups and downs of life, karmic awareness & change as my gift, and remove from this place illusion, deceptions & emotional imbalances.

In reading these oracles, perhaps we can hear the spirit of the Tarot telling us of its gifts, and perhaps we can consider each of the cards mentioned in a new light within a reading – as giving a gift or challenging an attachment.

With blessings and thanks to the living oracles of our Facebook group at:

http://www.facebook.com/groups/Tarotprofessionals/

We have given several kickstarts in this book to the relation of Tarot images to various facets of the spiritual life. In Magick, a more dynamic approach is taken to "cause change in conformity with will". Here we offer a brief and simplified form of ritual into which you may consider placing any work with your Tarot.

The practice of Ritual is a poorly appreciated part of our heritage. Ritual survives in our daily lives, but has become unconscious; our daily ritual of going to work, or the ritual of preparing a cricket pitch for play; a Punch and Judy show, the weekly rituals of the Lottery; and so on. Magical Ritual aims to perform a ritual as a dynamic, active, conscious event, to focus our intention and channel all available energies towards a specific goal.

Each element of a ritual represents a part of the process we are "acting out" within a defined area, the "temple". As such, each prop, movement and word becomes symbolic of the project we have chosen to magically empower by the ritual, be it a new job, a change of house, or a work of art.

The ritual "tools" also embody specific aspects of the environment around the magical worker, both the psychological and the physical universe. Although the tools have a variety of roles dependent on the rite, they can be basically seen as;

The Temple	the world around you.
The Circle	your own sphere of influence.
The Altar	the basis of your work in the world, the fixed point.
The Wand	your Will, or Energy.
The Cup	your Understanding of the situation.
The Sword	your Reason and Mind.
The Pentacle/Table	the Material with which you work.

Thus, when one drinks water from a cup and then walks towards the table, we are in effect saying, "I understand the situation I am in and now I know which things I need to work with in order to change the situation." By taking the Wand from the Table you further make known that you are to devote your energy and direction to making that change. All that in a simple series of actions!

Your location in the Temple during the ritual is also of significance, as the Temple floor is "invisibly" designed to represent the plan of the Tree of Life, and the other symbols which might be being worked. In some rituals, the symbol of the sign is actually drawn out on the floor of the Temple as a guide to movement throughout the ritual.

It is obviously important not to change any one part of a ritual without considering its relationship to a number of levels and systems into which it has been placed. The design of a ritual is a magical act in itself, and although there may be inharmonious elements left in the rituals due to attempting to weave diverse stands together, we must try to minimize them.

The ritual stages of purification, consecration, banishing and invocation serve to achieve the following ends, which are explained in further detail below,

Purification   Removes all elements in the environment antagonistic to your aims.

Consecration   Dedicates the remaining elements to the task in hand.

Banishing   Prepares yourself and defines the area in which you are working.

Invocation   Calls the forces and energies appropriate to the project at that point.

Purification

One purpose of the Purification is to ensure that the Temple is receptive to the forces which are to be invoked. You may have experienced going into a building or room and being struck by an oppressive atmosphere; this is the result of use for purposes which are emotionally charged, which has caused a build-up of the emotion in the fabric of the building and its location (such charges can outlive the building itself, if strong enough). All such places should be regularly purified by use of a simple technique such as this one. It is also possible for a building or room to pick up pleasant feelings, which can be equally strong. In such cases, purification seems to cleanse the room of specific associations without removing the atmosphere itself.

Strong emotional or purpose-specific contamination of a Temple can limit the effectiveness of later invocations - or even repel the influence altogether.

A second, equally important, function of Purification is to help develop a receptive state in the Celebrants. It is useful to focus on receptivity during the Purification in order to enhance this effect. Relax and encourage your mind to become dark, silent and still. In this way it will have the same effect on you as on the Temple.

Consecration

This is the active complement to Purification. Its function in the Temple is to complete the clearance of build-up, by forming an 'active readiness' to receive new influences.

Celebrants should also encourage this state in themselves during the consecration.

At the end of the Ceremony, the function of Purification and Consecration is to eliminate after-effects of the ceremony and ready the room for its next use.

Ritual Format

PURIFICATION

<sprinkle water>

Say: So therefore first the priest, who governeth the works of fire, must sprinkle with the lustral waters of the loud resounding sea.

CONSECRATION

<fumigate with incense>

Say: ... and when all the phantoms have departed, thou shalt hear the voice of the fire, that voice which darts and flashes throughout the hidden depths of this universe (from the Chaldean Oracles).

The Four Elemental Weapons

The first teachings of ritual are of the four elements, and their corresponding temple tools. You can also use the Four Aces of the Tarot to represent these tools. Each of the tools is a symbol of the elements and their basic correspondence to Nature.

All attributions commence in the East, the place of the Dawn, and complete in the North, the place of Earthing.

The Sword or Athame	Air	East	Clarity
The Wand or Staff	Fire	South	Will
The Cup or Chalice	Water	West	Depth
The Pantacle, Disk	Earth	North	Completion

To activate and recognise the four elements in your life, you can use your hand to call forth the four elemental weapons and their powers:

Palm facing Upwards: "This is my Pantacle, where my life is lived"
Palm Cupped: "This is my Chalice, where my love is lived"
Palm Sideways: "This is my Knife, where my decisions are lived"
Palm Sideways, one finger pointing, others under thumb: "And this is my Wand, where my Will is lived."

"My life is in my hands"

The power of Tarot to express the mystical experience was fully appreciated by A. E. Waite, whose first Tarot project with Pamela Colman-Smith has proven the most popular and de-facto setting for Tarot iconography for a century. We have illustrated and explored his much more profound and considered "second Tarot", executed by the stained-glass artist J. B. Trinick, in our book *Abiding in the Sanctuary* (Keswick: Forge Press, 2011).

In this second Tarot, Waite returns to depict the images as an ascent – a Christian ascent – of the human presence up the Tree of Life. In making this ascent, accompanied by the *Shekinah* (presence of God, usually depicted as feminine) the initiate eventually attains a state Waite terms *Unitas*, a sacramentalism of our inward nature.

Waite writes on this in his often overlooked *The Way of Divine Union* (1905), which was written just before he embarked on illustrating the path with the Waite-Trinick Tarot. His writing, whilst couched in Christian terminology, is suffused with highly emotive divine longing and mystical experience. He writes, "God is immanent within us but is asleep for us till we awaken Him, and it is often a work of many years to learn the secret of the quickening kiss. It is a secret of joy and tears" (p. 287).

In describing this path, Waite points out that it is indeed a personal path, unique to each of us; "The truth is that life is individual and to each therefore shall a path at his need be given" (p. 145). However, the road, no matter how travelled, and from whence commenced, is always the same; certain experiences are catholic in that words truest sense, "the developments differ, but it is the same in essential nature everywhere … the field of consciousness is without limit in its reception of experience, but it remains that which it is" (p. 147).

We would recommend this book by Waite to all those looking to understand his Tarot, particularly the Waite-Trinick images. The secrets of the Mystical Marriage and the Christ-Life are integral to his Tarot as a truly spiritual illustration and inspiration.

We will now recommend further reading for those wishing to explore various avenues of mysticism, personal work and magick through the auspices of each of the Major Arcana.

The Fool: *The Cloud of Unknowing*, Anon.

The Magician: *Magick in Theory and Practice*, Aleister Crowley.

The High Priestess: *Daughter of Fire*, Irina Tweedy.

The Empress: *Finding God in the Singing River*, Mark I. Wallace.

The Emperor: *The Fourth Way*, P. D. Ouspensky.

The Hierophant: *Meister Eckhart*, trans. Edmund Colledge & Bernard McGinn.

The Lovers: *The Crucible of Love*, E. W. Trueman Dicken.

The Chariot: *The Illusion of Conscious Will*, Daniel M. Wegner.

Strength: *Man's Search for Meaning*, Viktor E. Frankl.

The Hermit: *The Art of Contemplation*, Ramon Lull.

The Wheel of Fortune: *The Book of the Die*, Luke Rhinehart.

Justice: *Straight and Crooked Thinking*, Robert H. Thouless.

The Hanged Man: *Life in the Labyrinth*, E. J. Gold.

Death: *A Year to Live*, Stephen Levine.

Temperance: *The Book of Abramelin*, Georg Dehn.

Devil: *The Origins of Consciousness in the Breakdown of the Bicameral Mind*, Julian Jaynes.

Blasted Tower: *Prometheus Rising*, Robert Anton Wilson.

The Star: *I Hope I Shall Arrive Soon*, Philip K. Dick.

The Moon: *Meditation and Kabbalah*, Aryeh Kaplan.

The Sun: *A Separate God: Origins and Teachings of Gnosticism*, Simon Petrement.

The Last Judgment: *Global Brain*, Howard Bloom.

The World: *The Unfinished Universe*, Louise B. Young.

This is of course a nascent list for your own expansion. We have tried to present here a few avenues which may soon lead you to your own highways in the spiritual world.

Apostasis Spread

Whilst this book provides more in the way of contemplation and inspiration of ideas related to our approach to Tarot, we here offer a practical spread for significant change-work in your life. It is based on the concept of Apostasis, which refers to the end or crisis-point of a disease, usually by an expulsion of the dis-ease.

Here we see it in Campbell's context of the heroic journey, an archetypal pattern that plays out in all our lives, whether it is the epic saga of Beowulf, or an issue with one's Grendal-like boss at work. In any situation that requires a significant spiritual decision or life-style (and hence value-related) choice/impact, this spread can help give elegant and effective perspective.

This spread is a Tarosophy Split Deck method, in which we separate out Majors, Minors and Court Cards into three piles which are then separately shuffled and laid out.

First, shuffle the entire deck. Lay out the top card of the deck to your left, and the bottom card to your right as follows:

These are your Birth and Rebirth cards. They indicate what is already born from you, and what is required to initiate the next birth of a new self.

Then split out the remaining deck into three piles for the Majors, Minors and Court Cards.

Shuffle the Majors. Lay one down, this is your Calling.

Shuffle the Minors. Lay one down, this is the Threshold at which you stand.

Shuffle the Court Cards. Lay one down, this is the Temptation that leads you away from crossing the threshold to answer your calling.

Shuffle the Majors. Lay one down, this is your Return. This shows how you may make your journey beyond the rebirth. It offers advice and a form of hope for what lies for you after significant initiation.

Shuffle the Minors. Lay one down, this is your Rescue. It indicates what will be rescued within you from this particular initiation.

Shuffle the Court Cards. Lay one down, this is your Gift. It shows the character of your gift, which you can offer others, following this stage of your spiritual journey.

You can also select a card from any of the three piles to indicate "How Can I unite my Upper and Lower Worlds"?

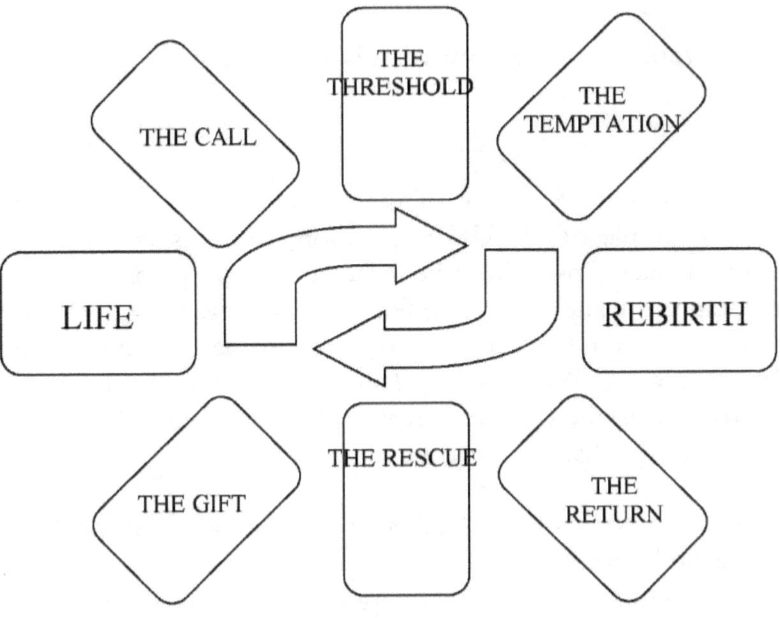

Illus. Apostasis Spread

Restoring a Spiritual Dignity to the Tarot

Truth is brief, (afterward, it is all commentary)

p. 633, *Foucault's Pendulum*

As was summarized in one of the appendices of *Tarosophy*, half a surveyed sample of the UK population, when asked about Tarot and other such "psychic" phenomena (including, bizarrely, Yoga and Satanism in the same list), felt that Tarot was "evil". That is to say, it represented some way of influencing the mind beyond "general advice". Whilst some Tarot readers may be forgiven for thinking this is their entire purpose, it is not one which is easily delivered to that half of the population.

It appears to us, that this signifies a common lack of respect for the practice and diverse beliefs of Tarot. There is a lack of dignity accorded to this profession or the pursuit of a passion in study.

The word **dignity** is an ambiguous word, in philosophical, ethical or legal terminology alike, so we will not attempt to offer more than our own usage of it. To us, it signifies a lack of respect to the individual who is practicing Tarot. We refer to the innate right of respect for one's pursuits, pleasures, passion or profession, whether you are a Tarot reader, student, sanitation officer or nurse.

That this dignity is not accorded to Tarot should be self-evident in most readers experience. Even at the most elegant and cultured dinner-parties, we have been subjected to "can you read these crisps if you haven't brought your cards" type routines. However, in personal experience we have found that adopting a non-apologetic "normalized" stance is the most effective in such situations.

And with regard to the "spiritual" dignity that the practice of Tarot and divination – a term which equates most nobly to *divinization* – may hold, we refer specifically to its use as a language for spiritual development. At one time, the project for Tarot was to imagine it as a grand scheme, a pictorial language, for the narrative of the soul's ascent. It was viewed as a picture-book of enlightenment.

That this spirituality was lost to rapid layers of magic, mysticism and enigmatic correspondence, scandal, dissension and other mundane manifestations, notably in the Golden Dawn society that introduced Tarot to those who then popularized it (Waite, Crowley, Colman-Smith, Foster-Case) is unfortunate. However, it is not irredeemable. The project of the Golden Dawn was to construct, in one of the three co-founders, William W. Westcott's words, a "complete scheme of initiation" – a curriculum - for an awakening of the "spiritual consciousness".

However you see that spiritual awakening, the Tarot was seen as a language for that landscape of mystical experience. It seems that the language is often taught, without any intent to visit the place in which that language is spoken. Whether we are performing a reading for "when will Dwayne come back to me" or our own self-development, we are participating in that larger landscape.

The Ascent Narrative illustrated as a Tarot journey

In the Order of the Golden Dawn, the Adeptus Minor hears this in their ritual of initiation;

> This is the symbolic mountain of God in the centre of the Universe, the sacred Rosicrucian Mountain of Abiegnus. Below and around it are darkness and silence, and it is crowned with the Light ineffable. At its base is the wall of Enclosure and Secrecy, whose sole gateway, invisible to the profane, is formed of the two pillars of Hermes. The ascent of the mountain is by the spiral path of the serpent of wisdom.

The Golden Dawn, Israel Regardie, p. 242

This "spiral path" weaves its way up the Tree of Life, to which are corresponded (on the paths) the Major Arcana, but within the Sephiroth, the Minors. These correspondences provide us a map of that ascent. However – we must remember at all times, it is only a map, and one of many.

Aldous Huxley writes,

> Even the most ordinary experience of a thing or event in time can never be fully or adequately described in words. The experience of seeing the sky or having neuralgia is incommunicable; the best we can do is to say "blue" or "pain", in the hope that those who hear us may have had experiences similar to our own and so be able to supply their own version of the meaning.

> To suppose that people can be saved by studying and giving assent to formulae us like supposing that one can get to Timbuctoo by poring over a map of Africa. Maps are symbols, and even the best of them are inaccurate and imperfect symbols. But to anybody who really wants to reach a destination. A map is indispensably useful in indicating the direction in which the traveler should set out and the roads that he must take.

> *The Perennial Philosophy* (p. 134)

A Map of the Spiritual Mountain in the Minors

When considering the spiritual levels of Tarot, the rich tapestry of the Majors can provide all the archetypal fabric we require to describe any profound vista of the soul. Toni Gilbert provides us a wonderful survey of the Majors for healing and spiritual growth in *Messages from the Archetypes* (Ashland: White Cloud Press, 2004) and briefly presents the Minor cards in two levels, an upper and a more "primitive" enactment of their archetypal energies. Madonna Compton deals only exclusively with the Majors in her *Archetypes on the Tree of Life: The Tarot as Pathwork* (St. Paul: Llewellyn, 1991).

So what of the Minors? What do they have to tell us about our spiritual path?

In a hermetic perspective, when arrayed on the Tree of Life, the Minor cards correspond with the four worlds and the ten *Sephiroth* —

four levels of ten descending (and ascending) energies. They run from the Ace down to the Ten, in each number descending from the Wands, through the Cups, Swords and finally to the Pentacles. These are the four worlds of Kabbalah, whose names are given here purely for reference:

Wands	World of Atziluth	Emanation
Cups	World of Briah	Creation
Swords	World of Yetzirah	Formation
Pentacles	World of Assiah	Action

Students of *Tarosophy* will recognize these four worlds as the four levels of Tarot card interpretation; literal (Assiah), symbolic (Yetzirah), extended (Briah) and secret (Atziluth).

We can also give the names of the Sephiroth and their numbers which provide a key-phrase together with the world (suit) in which that number sits, informing the nature of the card. This was expressly utilized by the Golden Dawn and Aleister Crowley in their Tarot.

10. Malkuth – Kingdom

9. Yesod - Foundation

8. Hod - Glory

7. Netzach - Splendor

6. Tiphareth - Beauty

5. Geburah - Strength

4. Chesed - Mercy

3. Binah - Understanding

2. Chockmah - Wisdom

1. Kether - Crown

So this allows us to see, through correspondence, that the Six of Pentacles is the "Beauty of Action" which gives a far deeper interpretation of that card in a reading. In taking these higher meanings, we can more easily apply them to even the most mundane of situations which are their lower reflection. Another example might be the 3 of Swords, which here is now the "Understanding of Formation", showing how that card depicts the painful realization that whatever is formed, is separate.

You can now go through the 40 Minors yourself and see how this generates meaning for the cards from these key words.

In this schema we commence with the Ace of Wands at the very highest level of divinity, descending all the way down through forty gates to the Ten of Pentacles, the grossest matter.

And here is the hermetic mystery enshrined more than ever — that "as above, so below". In Kabbalah it is said that "Kether is in Malkuth, and Malkuth is in Kether", and in Alchemy, "the heaven is in the earth, but after an earthly manner; and that the earth is in the heaven, but after a heavenly manner" (pp. 20-1, *The Kabbalah Unveiled*, S. L. MacGregor Mathers, London: Routledge Kegan & Paul, 1981).

So the Ace of Wands is the "creative beginning" of pure spirit (*Mastering the Tarot*, Eden Gray, New York: New American Library, 1971, p. 26) and the Ten of Wands is the card of "great financial stability" and final manifestation (p. 69). The forty gates of the Minors are arrayed between these poles.

Out of interest, in the extremes of this arrangement, when we see the upper world of the Wands in the lowest Sephirah, the Ten, there is "Ruin of all plans and projects. Complete disruption and failure" (Gray, p. 66). The highest Ace in the lowest world, Pentacles, is better dignified, for in it we see the "lilies of spiritual thought" growing in its garden (p. 29). Some suits (Worlds) support a better dignity to different ranges of number (Energy) in the context of this mapping.

In using this map of forty gates, we can plot a spiritual path up the flanks of Mount Carmel (see *The Interior Castle or The Mansions* by St. Theresa, and *The Mystical Doctrine* of St. John of the Cross) commencing our ascent with the Ten of Pentacles and aiming our vision on the Ace of Wands. We will first sketch out some of the significant points of this path by looking at the four Tens as our starting position, and then take a more detailed trip up the entire Tree in the highest world, the Wands. Firstly we will summarize the entire journey.

10 of Pentacles: It ends, as it began, in a garden. In our everyday experience, we are furtherest, yet closest to the light. As it is said, "the light shineth in the darkness, but the darkness comprehendeth it not". This card shows our sleeping state – and yet from this we can awaken, it is a full circle. The Gnostics say, "one by one, we are taken out of the world".

There is also a secret teaching embedded in this card as depicted by Waite and Colman-Smith. **The young child looking back out at us is he who grows up to be the Fool.** He clutches at the dog that will accompany him on his entire spiritual journey. It is his first (and last) attachment – faith. Whether you have faith in your family, friends, material wealth or wisdom, it is all the same in the Abyss – nothing. The child takes a white rose from this garden of matter in the 10 of Pentacles and at last gives it to heaven in the final card of the journey, the Fool.

As Waite says in describing the Fool, this is a cyclic process; "The sun, which shines behind him, knows whence he came, whither he is going, and **how he will return by another path after many days**" (p. 154-5, *Pictorial Key to the Tarot*).

10 of Swords: Our next step is that of realization of our intellectual attachments, and how these pin our body to the ground of matter. These too will have to be transcended in the "Great Work". The

card shows us how these inner voices fixate us and provide a mantra of attachment even in our most inner environment. There will be pain removing these inner voices, as many of them have been there for a long time.

10 of Cups: The illusion of happiness in attachment – we see here on closer examination that it is only a stage-set, a fiction. Some day that curtain will be drawn up, and nothing will be saved. The Sufis say, "you only truly possess what you would not lose in a shipwreck". It will take a great force of will to see through this façade.

10 of Wands: Here we see the highest expression of energy in the lowest world. We struggle constantly in a world of duality to meet our own expectations, values and standards. We are always working towards some goal or another, blindly and valiantly. Yet this is not the answer – the 10 must become the 1, those Wands must be pulled together and bound into one true thing, held not by ourselves but by the divine.

Here is the short-cut of initiation and mystical insight; that all that we fight is our false sense of self and all that arises from that mistake. Only we can lay our own burden down and release ourselves. As Da Free John simply says, "Avoiding relationship?"

We will now provide key concepts for the remaining cards in the spiritual ascent journey, demonstrating how they show a progressive development of the soul. Again, we know not if this were intended, nor does it particularly matter – we read the design as it is read. Those who study the initiatory system through Kabbalah will recognize the grade system experiences in these descriptions.

9 of Pentacles: The garden of security is now revealed; do we take off and fly or live in the uncomfortable knowledge that there is simply more than this to our lives?

9 of Swords: The constant shocks of life cannot be blanketed forever – and even if so, they lead to our death. No matter how painful, we must face the truth of our lives.

9 of Cups: Then we begin to see our own smugness, ego-games and in doing so, start to be removed from them – a quiet change begins in our awareness as we constantly observe our own emotional state.

9 of Wands: We begin to realize what is valuable to us, how our wounds have made us stronger – and how the world provides these opportunities constantly. We hold fast to an uncomfortable truth.

8 of Pentacles: The Worker is Hidden in the Workshop. We begin to conduct inner work and test our enquiries into the Universe and ourself, from a higher perspective. We may explore alternative spiritualities – the secret is to work, consistently, patiently and without pause. This is a card of service, as Jasmine Sim, a Tarot reader in Singapore says, "we continue to perfect the art and then we can share it with others".

8 of Swords: Until ultimately this begins to reveal what we know and what we don't know. We begin to see that all the traps and distractions were only of our own making – we have been playing a game which has become real, because it has been going on so long.

8 of Cups: So we walk away. Eventually we must act on our changing perspective of the world. The inner light eclipses the outer and we often find in this stage that we make major lifestyle changes, move home, career, relationships – it is always a difficult step.

8 of Wands: And a new energy comes, clean, fresh and rapid. A higher connection starts to move us, we feel enthusiastic about our course, borne aloft as if on the wings of angels. We may not at this stage know where we are going, but we know for sure that we are going.

7 of Pentacles: In Netzach now, we begin to pass into a phase of contemplation. We look at Nature as an exemplar and learn through Her teaching. The spell of the sensuous calls us to unity, a slow alchemy begins to take place in this long waiting game.

7 of Swords: Like a "thief in the night" our old ideas are becoming obsolete. Without any effort, they are taken from us, leaving only

what is congruent to our own personal experience. This is the Venusian Netzach undoing of the Mercurian Hod.

7 of Cups: There is an emotional upset at this stage for it feels like everything is possible and everything is permitted. When we are undone, what do we see – everything unraveled. However, as always, the secret is what transmutation is being wrought on our self – the only thing we cannot see. Here (in the Waite-Smith image) we become a shadow, and there is much at this time to be drawn from that shadow.

7 of Wands: Ultimately, this stage leads to an inner resolution. A stand. A statement that cannot be argued, from within, that enough is enough. We take our place for our role in the Universe and fill out the job description. Then we wait.

6 of Pentacles: And wait and wait. A new equilibrium takes centre stage and we begin to balance our own books – our resources, energies, we align to our highest vision. We seek only harmony, a divine balancing act, without knowing against what we are being judged nor what waits for us below or at the end of the rope.

6 of Swords: The only thing we can now do is take ourselves away from the world. It has nothing left to offer us, so we travel – literally or metaphysically – to new horizons. This is often inexplicable and unexplainable to others. It may begin to feel as if what we think we are is actually steering the course – and this is true.

6 of Cups: Through this middle stage, we are wed to our highest angel. It is like childhood, like widowhood, like a marriage, like death. It is the most significant stage of our spiritual progression and is called "the knowledge and conversation of the Holy Guardian Angel".

6 of Wands: And after a long honeymoon, we make our way back to the city, back to the noise, back to the people and the places. However, we are fundamentally changed – we have been somewhere and make our return anew.

5 of Pentacles: What follows in the spiritual journey – as seen through the Tarot and the initiatory system – is somewhat of a jolt. This is explained in Marcus's *After the Angel: An Account of the Abramelin Working* and many other mystical biographies. The 5 of Pentacles shows the banishment, the ejection, rejection, the excommunication of the self that is experienced at this stage following the ecstasy of the Angel. This is a dark night of the soul.

5 of Swords: Everything one thinks one knew is now stripped. Or flayed. "Eckhart saw Hell too. He said: The only thing that burns in Hell is the part of you that won't let go of life, your memories, your attachments. They burn them all away. But they're not punishing you, he said. They're freeing your soul. So, if you're frightened of dying and... and you're holding on, you'll see devils tearing your life away. But if you've made your peace, then the devils are really angels, freeing you from the earth." (*Jacobs Ladder*, 1990)

5 of Cups: In the desolation of the Wastelands, only Chapel Perilous awaits across the bridge. It is time to decide what is real and what is not, to turn one's back on the fictions of the former self and follow the Current of Creation. This is the time of great despair.

5 of Wands: In one's surrender to the Angel, and following from that event, values and spiritual concerns are utterly re-aligned, reformulated and re-established on a new system, a system not of oneself. The edifice of the self and all its relationships – the grand façade – is destroyed utterly and a new pattern of being arises. This equates to the grade of *Adeptus Major* in the western esoteric initiatory system.

4 of Pentacles: Whilst this may seem the most mundane of material images, Waite says succinctly, in *The Pictorial Key to the Tarot*, "He holds to what he has". To the spiritual journeyer at this stage, this simple mantra embodies a whole mystical approach to life. It is one demonstration of how a sentence can be given which means nothing at one grade, yet at higher grades takes on a knowing significance. The whole of Dion Fortune's *Mystical Qabalah* book is written in that same manner.

4 of Swords: The mental faculties now go into retreat and re-align themselves. The mystical quest alights in the sanctuary and reviews all that has arisen. There is a simple clarity, as of light passing through a stained-glass window, a "veil of vibrating light" as Trinick calls it. In that window (in the Waite-Smith Tarot) is the word PAX. This refers to *Chesed*, the fourth Sephirah and our present stage in the journey up the Tree, which means "Mercy".

4 of Cups: All temptations are now refused and one becomes utterly divine-sufficient rather than self-sufficient. This is the last of the challenges before the Abyss. There is only the Trinity ahead.

4 of Wands: The Abyss. There is no self on the other side of that invitation.

3 of Pentacles: Now within the Holy Sanctuary, the Master of the Temple commences work under new management.

3 of Swords: After fulfilling that work, the Mind (through that work, by which we are changed) becomes a tripartite form, with a heart that burns for the divine.

3 of Cups: The people must be celebrated and their causes uplifted to fulfill the spiritual duty. There is no self in this, only service.

3 of Wands: There is only a far horizon in sight, and all journeys now lead to divine service. In the clothing and head circlet of this figure (Waite-Smith Tarot) we see intimations of the Magician, who is the image of the archetype of spiritual service. We now take the step and commit ourselves to the light, whilst knowing even this is another journey, not the end.

2 of Pentacles: Again, in contrast to its usual mundane meanings, this card embodies in our spiritual light a far more profound teaching. It is significant of the action of "Chockmah" in the World of "Assiah", the "Wisdom of Action" which is the literal translation of those signposts. It is no more complex than that; this card signifies the ongoing wisdom-in-action of the Magus, the one who is existing in this eternal moment. As Crowley indicates, it is at this

point that the Lord of Karma takes notice, and one's books become audited and balanced in every moment. There is no cause-and-effect here, everything is connected now.

2 of Swords: In this upper silence, the mind is stilled and held in singular balance. Beyond meditation (see *The Hidden Teachings beyond Yoga* by Paul Brunton) and beyond contemplation, the mind is blind unto itself. The tide draws out, the sun is eclipsed; our emotional world is withdrawn and our awareness vanishes. There is a period of divine emptiness, a holy moment like no other – the house is now prepared for the masters return.

2 of Cups: And as is – and always was – promised, with nothing more than a touch, a kiss, a gesture, like the opening of a palm, the filling of a cup, the Great Secret is revealed. All that exists arises from that moment, this co-creation of soul and silence, man and woman, human and divine. The spirit and the flesh, all dualities are known by the one to arise in a third, a red winged lion, perhaps, atop the wand of healing and wholeness. And that lion, that sacred revelation, devours and consumes us utterly.

2 of Wands: So it comes to pass, the journey is complete. Only the realm of the archetypes awaits; the Aeons, the realms and circles and zones and Sephiroth as they are known only in creation. We stand inbetween the pillars with the world as it began, all possibilities unfolding, no attachment, no particular perspective. In many ways, this is the ultimate depiction of the spiritual journey in this card. This is the outward Fool card in right relation to the Apparent World card. And the only outward sign of the journey is the Rose and the Lilly entwined. It is done. Tetelestai.

The Four Aces now can be seen to embody the seeds of what G. I. Gurdjieff called the **Four Ways** or paths of spiritual enlightenment:

Ace of Pentacles: The Way of the Fakir – the mastery of attention through asana, or physical work such as Yoga, dance, trance-work, etc.

Ace of Swords: The Way of the Yogi – the mastery of self through mental discipline.

Ace of Cups: The Way of the Monk (or Nun) – who works with the affections and spiritualizes the emotional worlds of faith and love as their path.

Ace of Wands: The Way of Synthesis – perhaps this is the esoteric way, and was coined by Gurdjieff as his "Fourth Way" teachings.

Meanwhile Back at the Beginning of the End

Having seen how the Minors map our spiritual journey, we will return to take a look at the starting positions of each world, the four tens, to demonstrate how they reflect the four aspects of existence in four elements. This is the "Zelator" grade of the western esoteric initiatory tradition, where all work is done, and the beginning of the spiritual journey commences – by working through the lessons and transcending each of the attachments illustrated by these cards. We will also demonstrate how they each contain a trap and at the same time, their highest principle is also evident – "as above, so below".

10 of Pentacles

The unity of the ten becomes at one between the Ten and the Ace of Pentacles. The aim is to get beyond the obstacles of the earthly pentacles thrown along the path, these will trip you up if you pause to want. The child in the 10 of Pentacles grows up at last to become the Fool in the pack. Earthly riches make the world go round but you will be caught on that Wheel if you become attached or fall asleep in the garden of earthly delight.

10 of Swords

This is what I mean when I say I would like to swim against the stream of time: I would like to erase the consequences of certain events and restore an initial condition. But every moment of my life brings with it an accumulation of new facts, and each of these new facts bring with it consequences; so the more I seek to return to the zero moment from which I set out, the further I move away from it . . .

Italo Calvino

As Da Free John also puts it, "It is always already too late" to commence the journey. The moment of thought that enquiries is a paradoxical separation from which no unity can follow. This attempt to return to the "zero moment" of the Fool is also part of the journey of the Tarot.

It may seem that we move further from it, but in actual fact we are moving circularly towards it in our journey, winding our way up the slopes of the mystical mountain of initiation. The Ten of Swords warns of the inertia that will inevitably arise from prolonged mental fatigue, when surrender is due. There is no more working out to do, the swords of emotional anguish do weigh heavily but your worst fears have materialized into reality.

Acceptance is to be embraced and a still point resonates .There Is now the prospect of a new start and relief that will come when all turns full cycle. The old wounds of the battle of the swords from Ace to Ten are the very wounds that will heal and transform into the Ace of Swords.

A transmutation can occur. The World spins and the Fool steps into existence again and so the cycle goes on - Hallelujah! In fact, in the Tarosophy Tarot, the Outer Deck Fool contains this word, for 'Hallel' in Hebrew means "somebody who acts madly", and 'Jah' is "creator" therefore this uplift of the Fool is as Creator and the "madness" that is actually the transcendence of the reason. See George Fohrer. *Hebrew and Aramaic Dictionary of the Old Testament,* under הלל. Walter de Gruyter, 1973.

In summary of the Ten of Swords, to quote Einstein, "Logic can only take us from A to B, imagination can take us anywhere". Both of these dualisms have their traps, but from each we do (Swords) can (Pentacles), must (Cups) and will (Wands) escape.

10 of Cups

The nature of the cups is seen most evidently the Three of Cups, the *Mitwelt*, that is a 'co- world', where two figures are depicted, male and female, and a third entity that evolves, whether it is the creation of children, or the creation of creation. Perhaps the images on the card can correspond to the *Mitwelt* way of being, as it can personify many things; it is a growing changing entity.

The Three of Cups may contain the 'third entity' with the manifestation of the below. All your wants, desires and hopes, and these find their completion in the Ten of Cups.

Think about what you would like to have filling your ten cups. If you like, you may try shuffling the Major cards of the Tarot, and choose ten which can be read as filling the ten cups below. Ask what they symbolize for you, these archetypal energies in each of these ten emotional and spiritual contexts. Thus, you might pull the Hanged Man for Cup Three, "love of survival through community/society". This might suggest you are tasked to work from a different perspective whilst remaining in mainstream society. The phrase "be in the world but not of it" might come to mind.

Don't leave anything out, be all-inclusive (4 of Cups). Don't be afraid to let go of obsolete desires (5 of Cups). In doing so, you can honor your innocence authenticity whilst maintaining a mature perspective (6 of Cups). Also while selecting your ten cards do not be distracted by passing fancies only choose what has endured (7 of Cups). You will soon find yourself free of what has been and your past will rapidly be eclipsed by a future, and one worth walking towards (8 of cups). And in this making your choice - walking in the path of your own grail quest - there is true satisfaction (9 of Cups).

And in the healing power of love, each of the ten cups contains a gift of divine exploration, as depicted by the previous Cup cards, from Ace to Ten, all each within another:

Cup one contains love of coming into existence

Cup Two contains love of the divine breath

Cup Three contains love of survival through society (culture)

Cup four contains love of your very own existence

Cup five contains love of melancholy

Cup six contains love of nostalgia

Cup seven contains love of imagination

Cup eight contains love of your worth

Cup nine contains security

Cup ten contains love of family

All ten cups contain all you may ever need. Perhaps this explains why the 10 of Cups is the most spiritually idyllic image of human existence, it is indeed the idealized and realized Lovers card, that archetypal image played out in the real world. As leading astrologer and author Lyn Birkbeck commented "it will end as it began - in a garden".

We must absorb from the 10 of Cups; experience the osmosis effect of love and being loved.

The Indwelling of Ten Cups Exercise

Here is an exercise you might like to try; by placing the Ten of Cups by your bedside with the Ace of Cups, be aware of your emotions through that following day, then on the second night change the ace for the two, repeat this each night, until you have the nine and the ten of cups together.

You may find this simple exercise opens your spiritual heart quest, it a way of connecting that flow of the ace into the ten. The most powerful magic is when you invoke the highest into the very far reaches of what is below.

If you are interested in exploring more about the Path of Love, including how transference, 'threeness', and even Kaballah relate to this journey, see chapter 11, 'Love's Angel', in *Pilgrimage of the Heart: The Path of Romantic Love* (Haule, 1992).

10 of Wands

This is the highest level of energy dropped into the lowest world; it shows what Crowley called "the force detached from its spiritual sources". For us in our quest to redeem our own spiritual dignity, this card shows the worst result of misunderstanding the spiritual path. As Crowley says "The whole picture suggests oppression and repression. It is a stupid and obstinate cruelty from which there is no escape. It is a Will which has not understood anything beyond its dull purpose, its 'lust of result', and will devour itself in the conflagrations it has evoked" (pp. 194-5, *The Book of Thoth*). Where we see these characteristics in a person or a situation we know that it is far removed from spiritual dignity, which is ultimately characterized by the Ace of Wands.

The Spiritual Journey in the Wands

So from each of the Tens we can commence our spiritual journey as we have seen through the entire 40 Minors. Let us finally work through the Wands as a more detailed example and each see how they re-connect us when we feel lost from our spiritual source. You can recreate this detailed mapping with each of the other suits to show the way out of any dilemma in any world from a spiritual point of view. If you constantly struggle with your relationships, family and emotions, examine this journey in the Cups, if your finances and material work, the Pentacles, and if your education and thinking, the Swords.

10 of Wands

We begin by observation of where we struggle to "be spiritual". This is always our first signpost. The spiritual path is characterized by the wrestling with one's own Angel. There is always something more which must be discovered, always something presently preventing us being in the moment. The Ten of Wands calls us to step away from the struggle. Where we have patterns in our life that constantly weigh us down, these are each a potential Ace of Wands, repeating time and again to awaken us. That person in the Ten of Wands is carrying ten identical Aces, they just do not realize it.

See Michal Conforti's *Field, Form and Fate: Patterns in Life, Nature and Psyche* (2003) for a fascinating exploration of how patterns in our life collaborate creatively to provide us opportunities for growth.

9 of Wands

So we begin with Burden of attachment, so we must let this go, it literally does not (is not) matter. We stop struggling and embrace our own wounds, as that is where we may become strong. We take it from the perspective that the process of scar formation and its life-long legacy is a protective mechanism to heal and protect us after harm. However after repair we are still 'vulnerable', as the replacement scar tissue is more fragile than our original tough skin; therefore, we need to be kind to ourselves and tread with care along the journey, and wisely choose who we entrust to help us to heal, whether it is friends, family, therapist or foe! It is tempting in emulating the Nine of Wands to 'Tread carefully and carry a big stick'.

From a Jungian perspective, the 'wounded healer' does not mean a 'once wounded now recovered' one, but one who is currently vulnerable as well (the latin word 'vulnus' means "wound"). We continue with our battle scars and wash them in the cave of wounds at dawn – a phrase that can be ritualized in the practice of the Greek mystery rites.

The Nine of Wands can illustrate the impact of childhood wounds on our adult self, which in turn affect the way in which we develop our own unique spiritual path. As one therapist said, "we cannot choose our garden, merely the way in which we work with it".

This aspect of the Nine of Wands can be explored in *Strong at the Broken Places* by Linda Sanford (1991). Whilst this book illustrates the quite rightfully so-sensitive aftermath of the effects of child abuse/neglect, it is written from the perspective of how the wounded (vulnerable) become empowered and it refutes the belief of some that the abused must become the abuser. It is an essential book for those working in any therapeutic modality.

The Nine of Wands teaches us that it is possible to escape our past. Or in the present moment "You do not have to attend every argument to which you are invited".

8 of Wands

At this point, escaping from our own past, we must not stop. This card tells us to keep going, to ride the energy from whatever source it is conjured. Think of the power of lightning and the strength that it wields. As Eco says, "Initiation is learning not to stop".

7 of Wands

Once we have begun on our journey, we must learn to use a spiritual system or map to maintain equilibrium.

6 of Wands

In engaging with a system, exploring it fully and deeply, dynamic energy brings new victories of understanding, taking one forward into new situations and states of being. We must be careful here for "pride cometh before a fall".

5 of Wands

At the next point, the inner work must be transformed into outer work. We exert great effort in a group to create and construct what is new and innovative. The way of the Five of Wands is "Just do it, go on get on with it NOW". Alterations can be made later; this stage is a production in progress. It is characterized in our spiritual life by constant change, challenge and growth, constant success and disappointment, a rapid realignment of one's values from moment to moment. It can lead to a new cohesive pattern or a complete breakdown.

4 of Wands

At last we achieve a form of stable inner Sanctuary, a place where you can consolidate your efforts so far, putting down tools for a while and rewarding yourself for your endeavors. This is also the stage in our quest termed by Robert Anton Wilson "chapel perilous", a phrase that originally occurs in Sir Thomas Mallory's *De Morte De Arthur*. It is the point in our spiritual journey where we have to decide whether we are being accompanied by a presence external to ourselves or choose to believe that it is all in our imagination. This card calls for an act to faith from which there is no return.

Those that make the wrong choice here – for choice it is – through fear (an incomplete initiation of their previous stage, the 5 of Wands) become what Crowley refers to as "Black Brothers". Whilst an admitted over-dramatization, this can be seen in anyone whose *modus operandi* is to cast doubt, confusion or dismay, to sow seeds of despair, to attract others to their cause. It is characterized by constant implicit calls for self-validation and ultimately (for its fault is to not be creative beyond its own delusion) implodes, taking those who have been attracted to its apparent delights with it.

3 of Wands

Having escaped the perils of the previous stages in our spiritual quest, the Three of Wands awaits. This is the stage where we have to think about where we are going next. We have turned our back on the past and look to the future, we cannot afford to be held back by restless yearning for old ties, and the new world is where the future of change lies. Do not find yourself left behind while others progress, avoid isolation. We have to pass on the baton. At its highest level this card signifies the trinity, generation, creation, progression/procession, all unified in one creative act.

This is best put by Maria Prophetissa, a 3rd century alchemist; "One becomes two, two becomes three, and out of the third comes the one as the fourth".

2 of Wands

The journey now nears its terminus with this Minor card combination of the upper level archetype cards of the World and the Magician. This signifies that the act of spiritual transformation is now out of our hands – whilst at the very same time we feel that all is within us. This is the "final ambush" that lies in wait for the journeyer in the spiritual realms. We have to discard all that might accumulate on this way, which is a *via exhaustio*, a "way of exhaustion":

> Thence the human being rushes up through the cosmic framework, at the first zone surrendering the energy of increase and decrease; at the second evil machination, a device now inactive; at the third the illusion of longing, now inactive; at the fourth the ruler's arrogance, now freed of excess; at the fifth unholy presumption and daring recklessness; at the sixth the evil impulses that come from wealth, now inactive; and the seventh zone the deceit that lies in ambush.

> Brian P. Copenhaver, *Hermetica* (Cambridge: Cambridge University Press, 1992) p. 6. See also Salaman, van Oyen, Wharton & Mahé, *The Way of Hermes* (London: Duckworth, 1999) p. 23

Ace of Wands

At last we come to the aim of our spiritual journey in the Wands. The value system of our whole being is taken in the hand of the divine. Compare this to where we commenced, with those ten rods on our own back, and we perceive the total exchange carried out in the journey. We have done nothing more than returned to the singular truth of the matter. We were never ourselves to begin with.

For more on the Initiatory Journey through the Tarot, you may wish to also read *The Element Tarot Handbook: Initiation into the Key Elements of the Tarot* by Naomi Ozaniec (Shaftesbury: Element, 1994).

For more on the wounded healer, see the bibliography and *Strong at the Broken Places*, Linda T. Sandford, London: Virago Press Ltd, 1991. Also, *The Wounded Healer: Countertransference from a Jungian perspective*, David Sedgewick, Hove: Routledge, 1994.

Illus. Mons Philosophourum from *Secret Symbols of the Rosicrucians from the 16th and 17th centuries*

> Thus then, my son, stand in a place uncovered to the sky, facing the southern wind, about the sinking of the setting sun, and make thy worship; so in like manner too when he doth rise, with face to the east wind.

The Hymnodia (from the *Hermetica*)

In these four exercises, which are carried out over a full year — marking the Solstices and Equinoxes - you will learn how to apply Tarot to create subtle and profound change in your life. The connection of the Sun to the spiritual life is profound, and aligning ourselves to its course is a common spiritual practice. It can be found in as varied practices as the Yogic Salutation to the Sun, the Hermetic *Hymnodia*, and the observations of *Liber Resh* in western esotericism.

The shifts of awareness in this practice will be created by using the correspondences of Tarot to large-scale events in the Cosmos itself, binding you into the largest cycles of life and nature. As you create these alignments for yourself, you will experience the "invisible knots" through which the world is created, both in time and out of time.

This may lead to spiritual insight, significant events in your life or subtle shifts creating a more harmonious and integrated environment for yourself and those around you.

In this first lesson, commencing at the Winter Solstice, we will introduce the idea of the Tarosophy *Heliakos*, and present our first exercise to prepare us for the Spring Equinox lesson which will follow on March 21st.

The Tarosophy Heliakos

The word Heliakos is the Greek origin of the word helical, and means simply "of the sun". In this Tarosophy working we work with the sun at four points of the earth's real-world orbit. Using correspondences to the Tarot we create a mirror of these four stations in our own life, aligning ourselves to Nature in a profound manner, both spiritually and practically.

The Tarot Precession

When the earth's orbit takes it closest and furtherest from the sun, we experience the shortest, longest, and two equal-length days and nights. These are the Solstices and Equinoxes. There is a Summer and Winter Solstice, and a Spring and Autumn/Fall Equinox.

Due to the precession of the equinoxes – a technical issue which we won't go into here, but do feel encouraged to research – the signs of the Zodiac in which the sun appears placed has changed over time. This means that the signs in which the sun appeared at the four stations of the Solstices and Equinoxes has also changed over time.

So, the traditional/prior positions of the Sun at these four times was:

Spring Equinox	March 21st	Aries
Summer Solstice	June 21st	Cancer
Autumn Equinox	September 21st	Libra
Winter Solstice	December 21st	Capricorn

And for example, using the calendar for 2011:

The dates on which an equinox and solstice falls are not always precisely on those dates, for 2011 the dates are as follows: March 20th (23:21 UTC), June 21st (11:28 UTC), September 23rd (03:09 UTC), December 21st (23:38 UTC).

We can now take a look at our Tarot card correspondences for these positions of the sun, using the Golden Dawn system of correspondences. We take the Major cards that correspond to those signs of the Zodiac, and discover that they are:

Spring Equinox	Aries	EMPORER
Summer Solstice	Cancer	CHARIOT
Autumn Equinox	Libra	JUSTICE
Winter Solstice	Capricorn	DEVIL

You may also note that these four Major cards also now become useful timing cards in a reading. You can either read them as exact dates or corresponding to that stage of an expected time sequence.

As an example, if you had the Devil as the Outcome card in a reading about a house sale, and the person had said they would have to take it off the market within a year if it didn't sell, the Devil card may show that they will have to wait all the way until the end (winter solstice equivalent) of that year for their outcome, even if that was the spring, being a year away from the reading.

However, the precession of the equinoxes has given us new signs, and hence new cards, for where these stations now fall.

These new positions and their cards are:

Spring Equinox	Pisces	MOON
Summer Solstice	Taurus	HIEROPHANT
Autumn Equinox	Virgo	HERMIT
Winter Solstice	Sagittarius	TEMPERENCE

You can see that these are very different cards indeed, and give us a novel Tarot Precession, where the cards, images, symbols and meanings that once applied for almost two thousand years to a time of year are now radically different.

We will use this observation to now re-align ourselves to the new scheme! We take the magical perspective that by doing this in a ritualistic and small-scale fashion; we will bring about corresponding changes in our environment and personal perspective.

WINTER SOLSTICE

The Tarot Precession Layout

So, to make this alignment to the new cosmology, and apply it in
your life, take the old and new cards out of the Majors and lay them
out as below.

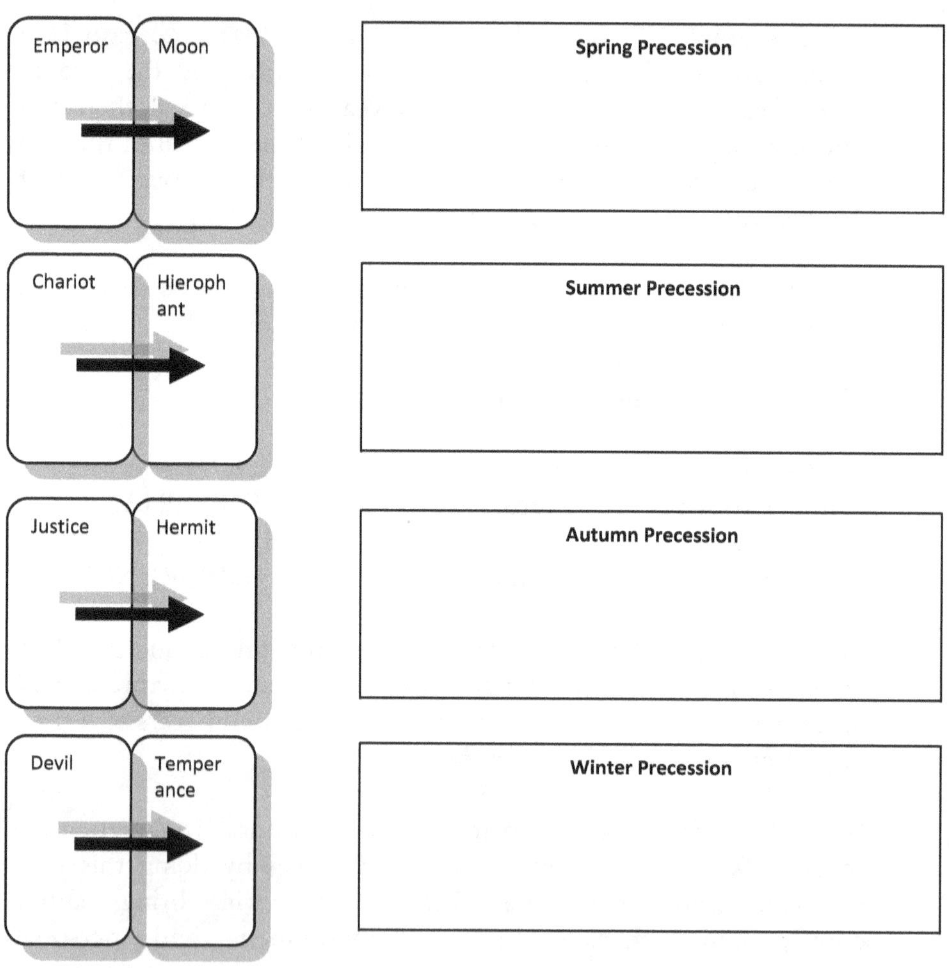

Creating your own Precession

To create your own alignment we need to consider the paired cards for each seasonal event. We take what we know of their meanings and apply these to our own lives. We then make notes in the appropriate boxes above to ensure that we then engage changes in our lives according to what we have divined from the layout.

Your Precession Cards

We will look in the following lessons over the year how we apply these changes, but for now, at the Winter Solstice, we will already be engaging change by considering the cards. We will give some examples below, but you are also encouraged to come up with your own "precessions" based on your understanding of the cards.

When we consider the paired cards, we look how the first card is an "outworn" or old pattern, being replaced by the second card as the "incoming current" or new way of behavior. Whilst this applies to the very grand scale of the stars, sun and earth, it also applies to our own lives. We then consider this change and list activities we can do to engage that change, even on the smallest scale, no matter what our resources. In doing so, we make an alignment with powerful effects on every level of existence. It is like a tuning fork, vibrating to a particular frequency which then makes everything around it vibrate to that same pattern.

So taking the Spring Precession first, we have:

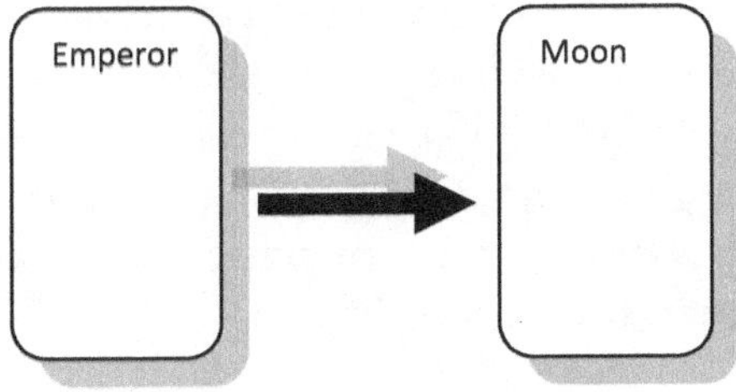

Using keywords, or a system like we describe in *Tarot Twist*, we come up with meanings for the two cards as: Emperor = Nurture/Power, and Moon = Reflection/Identity. So we consider that the precession is from old patterns of taking control, to new ways of being ourselves. We might write in the box for this pair, "How can I be myself without controlling others?" and list several new ways – almost like new year's resolutions, but reflecting a cosmological shift in the very stars themselves!

We can do this for all four events and start working on them now, as the next lesson will be a different experience building on what we have just done here. The more you make the changes and engage in actions according to this layout, the more impact it will have as we work through the three other stations.

We will quickly look at the other three pairs as below, and you can also discuss this in the Heliakos group on Tarot Town.

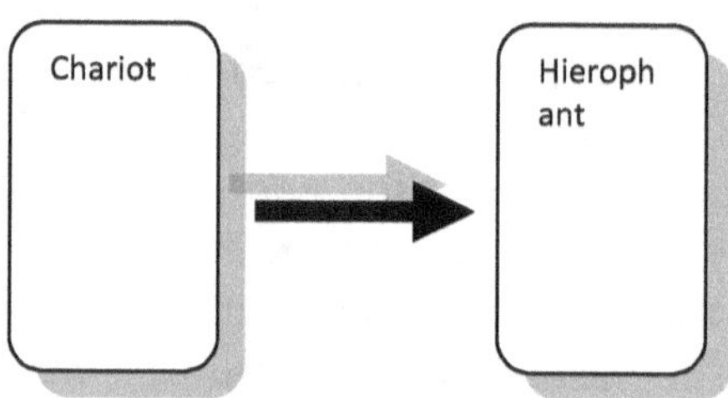

In *Tarot Flip*, we analyzed many experienced Tarot card readers unconscious meanings of cards, and discovered that most attribute Momentum to the Chariot and Teaching to the Hierophant. If we use those unconscious keywords for these cards, we see the precession as from activity and movement to transmission, of teaching, passing on wisdom. So the question for our activity for this precession could be "What can I teach (and how) from what has carried me to this point?" An answer might be to carry out some volunteer mentoring work, or write a Blog about something that gave you momentum in your life.

Our next pair is Justice to the Hermit, the Autumn Equinox precession. So if Justice has been replaced with the Hermit, what might this mean to us in our own lives? It might suggest that external law and legality is being replaced by a more personal and self-reflective ethical code. So our activity for this precession in our life might be "How can I do what is right for me whilst supporting the rights of others?" Perhaps join or make a small contribution to a campaign in which you believe or have personal experience.

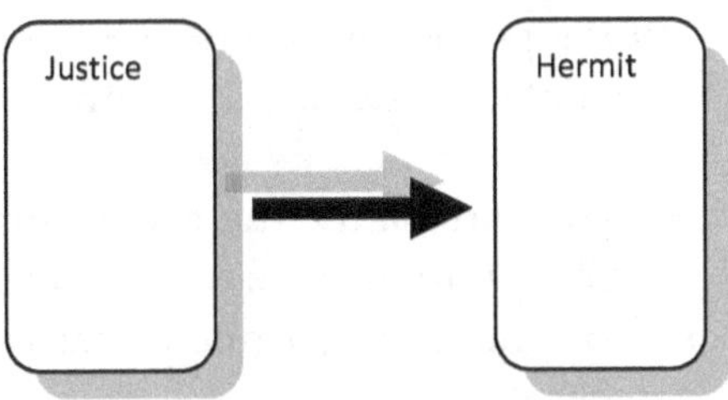

You will see that be enacting and engaging all four stations, all four precessions, you will come to make significant changes in your life, and they will have a culminating effect that will add up to more than the sum of the individual parts. This is the true magick of Tarot to picture powerful patterns of which we can take advantage in our lives. It is a method of spiritualizing our lives.

Our final station is the Devil to Temperance. This shows a powerful precession from temptation and excessive self-indulgence to moderation and self-control.

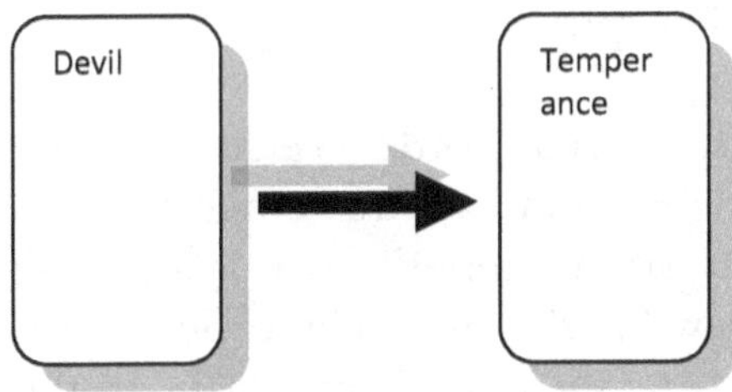

We might ask of this pair, in our own lives, "Where can I begin to harness my enthusiasm and attraction to certain things in my life into a more creative, productive and powerful agent?" You might consider looking at this precession pair in the Thoth Tarot by Aleister Crowley and Frieda Harris.

In fact, all of these four pairs may benefit from being examined in different decks to give you a full range of interpretations for your precessions.

The concept of Tarot precessions is one unique to Tarosophy and we hope that you find it a powerful experience to engage the model of Tarot in your spiritual life, producing a wealth of positive change.

As the year continues, you can follow the three further lessons each quarter to take this concept to new areas of your life and make transformations based on the most cosmic patterns in the universe, depicted in our little deck of cards.

SPRING EQUUINOX

The Tarot of the Invisible Temple

At this second station we celebrate and sanctify the **Spring Equinox**. You will have worked upon the precessions of the year since the Winter Solstice, and perhaps made some observations and adjustments in your outlook and behavior as a result. Once aligned to the cosmic scale of precession, we can take our part in the current as it flows invisibly in life.

The Tarosophy Temple

The Golden Dawn occult order celebrated the Equinox as a transition of the light. They saw this embodied in their Hierophant (literally, "revealer of mysteries"), who was re-installed at each Equinox with a new "password". The officers of each station were also re-consecrated to their respective tasks in the temple. As our temple is real life, and our hierophant is our Tarot deck, we have the Tarosophy Temple in our hands.

In this working, having passed through the precessions, we will create a new "word" for our journey between Equinox and Solstice, which embodies our own personal current of life. This will allow us to make easy progress in the tasks and projects we set ourselves, and may even produce strong synchronicities that take you even further than you thought.

We will then re-consecrate our Tarot in a ritual fashion to provide us guidance over this time of working in a real-life living temple of Tarot.

The Hierophant Takes Position

Take the Hierophant card out of a deck and place it someone where it can remain undisturbed. The Hierophant is an interface or communicator of the divine mysteries.

Take your deck and split it into the four suits and the majors.

Place the suits into four piles about the Hierophant, with each suit saying as appropriate:

I lay down the Suit of Pentacles, my attachments.
I lay down the Suit of Wands, my spiritual goals.
I lay down the Suit of Cups, my emotions.
I lay down the Suit of Swords, my thoughts.

Say LIGHT IS IN THE DARKNESS.

You may wish to light a candle at that point.

Shuffle the Major Cards and select four whilst contemplating the Hierophant.

Lay these out from right to left in front of the Hierophant card.

Use the key below to construct your "magical word" from the corresponding Hebrew letters for the time until the Summer Solstice.

Aleph	FOOL	A
Beth	MAGICIAN	B
Gimel	PRIESTESS	G
Daleth	EMPRESS	D
Heh	EMPEROR	H
Zain	LOVERS	Z
Cheth	CHARIOT	Ch

Teth	STRENGTH	T
Yod	HERMIT	Y
Kaph	WHEEL	K
Lamed	JUSTICE	L
Mem	HANGED MAN	M
Nun	DEATH	N
Samekh	TEMPERANCE	S
Ayin	DEVIL	A'a
Peh	TOWER	P
Tzaddi	STAR	Tz
Qoph	MOON	Q
Resh	SUN	R
Shin	LAST JUDGEMENT	Sh
Tau	UNIVERSE	Th

Your Magical Password

For example if you selected TOWER, STRENGTH, WHEEL & FOOL your magical word would be Peh + Teth + Kaph + Aleph, PTKA.

There is no guide to pronounce your word, you will have to decide!

The Hierophant is Throned

Having discovered your magical word and using the cards themselves as a reading, you can now take up your magical weapons again, i.e. the four suits.

Take up each suit and shuffle them back into a full deck with the Majors, saying:

I take back my Pentacle, blessed in light; in the name [say your magical word]

I take back my Wand, blessed in light; in the name [say your magical word]

I take back my Cup, blessed in light; in the name [say your magical word]

I take back my Sword, blessed in light; in the name [say your magical word]

Shuffle the entire deck and then place the Hierophant back in the deck saying:

The Hierophant is re-established in the new light of the Equinox, in the invisible temple.

Aligning to the Spring Current

To activate this current in your day, at any time over the next quarter you should take out the Hierophant from your deck and repeat your "magical word" several times strongly. You may even use your craft skills to place the magical name on an object, clothing, talisman, etc. Leave the Hierophant somewhere visible where the card will not be disturbed until you experience a strong "revelation", surprising helpful event or acceleration in your plans, or synchronicity. Then return the Hierophant to the deck.

You may wish to try this exercise 3-4 times during the quarter dependent on events.

We hope you experience some of the profound magical experiences that Tarot can bring about when aligned to the cosmic cycles, the deeper currents, the invisible knots and your everyday life together. The deck is a truly magical device and by activating it with ritual you will explore further of its many mysteries.

SUMMER SOLSTICE

The Labyrinth of the Sun

At the Summer Solstice, corresponding to the sign of Taurus, and the Hierophant of the Tarot, we make our way to align our solar course to what we call the Solar Labyrinth. In myth, this was where the Minotaur was held by King Minos. The labyrinth was constructed by Daedalus, who of course was the father of Icarus.

We are familiar with Icarus, who flew too close to the sun, and in doing so became an icon of failed ambition or hubris. He was also warned by his father not to fly too close to the sea below, as the salt would also damage his wings.

When we make our alignment at the Summer Solstice, we use our cards to provide a golden thread through the labyrinth, so we may continue our spiritual journey without losing ourselves to fear (our Minotaur) or pride (our Icarus).

You will need a "spare" deck for this exercise as it cannot be used for anything else between the Summer Solstice and the Autumn Equinox.

Contemplate the labyrinth and walk your eyes through it whilst shuffling the deck at the summer solstice. Imagine that this is an image of your life, moving to a hidden centre. In that centre is a golden bull, a solar statue, radiating light.

When you arrive at this centre, stop shuffling the deck and lay it down. If you have a separate image of the labyrinth, you can lay your deck face-down in the centre of it.

Leave the deck for a day from the Summer Solstice – go enjoy the day and its length from dawn to sunset.

The following day, take the bottom card of the deck out and turn it up – this is your "Sea". Take the top card out turn it face up – this is your "Sun". Lay out these cards above (Sun) and below (Sea) the labyrinth or on your table. For one week contemplate these two cards as the extremes of your spiritual course. What extremes must you avoid, how do you know you are going off-track or getting lost in the labyrinth of life?

If, for example, I had the 5 of Wands above, and the 3 of Cups below, this might indicate that I tended to get lost on my spiritual journey whenever I was involved in arguments or discord of values, or attempting to get others to do something practically without providing a vision. This is where I might tend to get "burnt".

The 3 of Cups below, for example, would tell me that I should also avoid dropping too low into the need for celebrating my own life, as this would corrode (salt) my spiritual wings.

After a week, leaving the rest of the deck in place, you can now use the deck as an "Ariadne's Thread" throughout the remaining quarter, until the Autumn Equinox. Any time you feel adrift or lost in the labyrinth, simply turn over the next card from the top of the deck. This will provide you a spiritual thread between the two extremes of life. If you wish, you can use this deck as your "card of the day" – a practice we generally avoid, however here it speaks to a deeper current in a wider context.

AUTUMN (FALL) EQUINOX

At the Autumn Equinox, we find our spirit resting from the light, entering into a transition phase prior to the dark of winter. The Autumn Equinox is all about portents of change.

Corresponding to Virgo, the Hermit, we see in the *Heliakos* that nature is our teacher; she shines the light from the mountains and the stars, to guide our path into the upper realms of darkness and silence, where there are no words.

Our alignment for this season becomes one of transition, being responsive and alert to all portents of change. It is a very simple technique, for we do not work during this time, but merely observe.

The Leaves of Autumn

Take your deck and shuffle it on the evening of the Autumn Equinox. Imagine that it is 78 leaves of the Tree of your Life.

Again, you will need to dedicate (consecrate) a deck for use only for this exercise for the following quarter.

When you feel that the deck has come to rest, simply take the top card out and use it to answer a simple question;

"Underneath everything, what is changing?"

Contemplate and if you wish, journal, your response.

Place the card back and shuffle again.

Leave the deck until you next require to ask the same question.

Repeat the shuffle, the drawing of a card, the return of the card and the shuffle.

Over the quarter, return to this exercise when you wish, always asking the same question. It is one of the rare occasions when it is worth repeatedly asking the same question of your Tarot.
The cycle then continues back to the Winter Solstice, where we examine the precessions in our spiritual life, and continue the spiral dance of the sun.

As with many of our longer and more advanced exercises, it may be that you only perform this process once, although you'll discover that repeating it may give new insight on progressively higher levels.

In this section we provide a series of spreads from our Tarot-Town social network site (www.Tarot-town.com) which has proven very popular. It is an example of what Tarosophy calls a "gated spread", a series of spreads that are linked by real-world activity. Each spread over the period of time (usually a week) within a gated spread depends on some activity to be carried out from the previous spread. This ensures that you are gearing the Tarot to "engage life, not escape it" throughout the experience.

As participants report significant events and even changes of life and inner experience through these immersive events, we would like to provide here our beginner version, the Tarot Shaman.

A Shaman is often a wounded healer, called to their vocation through illness or strange events in their early life. Whilst varying in practice and belief, they most often function as an intermediary between the mundane and the spiritual world.

The responsibilities of an Inner Shaman are:

- o To maintain a connection between the Lower and Upper Worlds.

- o Tap uncommon knowledge for socially useful purposes

- o Application of critical judgement to vision

- o To apply new guiding myth to changing circumstances

- o To alter a myth that is failing

After Feinstein & Krippner (1988).

The Tarot Shaman

As we have introduced, what follows are spreads arrayed across a period of time, where each spread is reliant not only upon the previous spread – but on actions carried out in real life (and arising results) which feed into the next spread. Thus a series of "gates" are created through which the activity of life is channelled. As the cards represent fundamental patterns in life, this channelling produces often profound life-changing effects beyond the obvious connectivity of life. It is a way of fully experiencing that the world is indeed "bound by invisible knots".

The Gated Spreads already taught within Tarot Professionals include one of Relationships – the Gates of Valentine week, one on Creativity – the Garden of Forking Paths, and the powerful Resurrection Engine – a totally life-changing week experience. You can discover more about this method and many other spreads such as the Palace of the Phoenix (using Alchemy) and the Temple of Thoth (using the Thoth deck and Egyptian mythology) at http://www.gatesofTarot.com.

In this Gated Spreads we are going to take a gentler journey into the animal symbolism of Tarot and engage with the living life with which we are surrounded. Indeed this may be a powerful week – whilst first writing up this whole exercise I looked out the library window and saw a Deer staring back in at me.

The Shaman

In the *Teachings of Don Juan*, Carlos Castaneda gives an account of the requirements of the Shaman, the Person of Knowledge. The Shaman must be:

1. Learned

2. Of Unbending Intent

3. Clear of Mind

4. Laborious

5. A Warrior

6. Unceasing

7. Possess an Ally

Whilst we see that the Tarot cards of the Magician, the Chariot, the Hermit, Strength, Emperor and the Wheel may symbolize the archetypal qualities of the first six of these qualities, we may also need to locate an Ally – in this case, the Spirit of the Tarot itself, to guide us further. But first we must encounter the Dweller on the Threshold – the Guardian of the Gate.

You may like to note in your journal which cards you personally see associated with the first six qualities that Castaneda gives for a Shaman. You may also like to record your dreams during this week which will often become more vivid.

Gate 1: The Guardian of the Gate Spread

Our first Gated Spread tells us what we must overcome to go onto the next gate – it is a warrior's challenge. We cannot even begin to approach the mysteries unless we prove ourselves in some serious manner.

So for your first Gate, take a deck and shuffle, considering everything that frightens you, then lay out 3 cards in a line (vertical or horizontal) as follows:

1. What is the Guardian?

2. How must I Fight?

3. What is the Reward?

Take these three cards and consider how they might relate to your life over the next day. What is the nature of the "fear" that has been divined by the first card? What is the manner in which you must overcome this fear indicated by the second card? What does the third card suggest you will gain as a reward?

I take out these cards in my reading:

1 Guardian – The Blasted Tower

2 Fight – Ace of Swords

3 Reward – Empress

I guess I start to see the Guardian as a fear of disruption and sudden failure. The fight is keeping clear to an idea, and the reward is a general natural growth.

Now – most importantly, decide on a definite ACTION tomorrow that will meet the requirements of this gate. Something in your life – not too dramatic unless you feel called to do so – that will respond to the divination of these three cards. It must be enacted within the following day.

So I decide in my case that tomorrow, Saturday, I will try and do something extremely surprising, that fits to my ideas, I'll overturn an expectation and overcome a barrier by starting to write an essay I have been prevaricating over. It's not much of a challenge in terms of being a warrior, but I'll determine to do it. The Ace of Swords!

You are encouraged to share your decisions, actions and experiences on our Tarot-Town forums, but only if you wish to do so. We have found in previous gated spreads that sharing often reveals profound similarities and interesting differences in the lives of those sharing the experience.

We will then be given the next Gate by the Tarot Shaman below and continue our journey into the Tarot Shaman's Path and meet our animal guide in the Tarot, having proven our worth at the first Gate.

The Tarot Shaman II

There are many forms of shamanistic practice and at the end of this week of the Tarot Shaman Gated Spread we will provide a reading list for those who wish to know more about Shamanism worldwide, from the archaic to the contemporary! Whilst there is no particular connection between Shamanism and Tarot, many of the methods and approaches found in shamanistic practice can be applied to deepen our experience of Tarot in a profound and practical way.

The Journey

In this next gate, having overcome the Guardian, we go on a journey to meet our Animal Guide. Of course, we must travel but we must also do so in a relaxed attitude – the world is closer to us than we imagine! There is a great scene in the book based around a re-imagining of Anglo-Saxon shamanism, *The Way of Wyrd*, by Brian Bates, where the shaman is taking a student through an exercise – he says; "Relax! You are tying yourself in knots with tension. Relax and your Guardian Spirit will cut through the fog of your life like a sunbeam". He then jokes that the student must have been chosen by an Owl guardian as he is looking so wide-eyed and intent! Humor is an important part of Shamanistic training, as is trickery!

So in our second day of the Tarot Shaman, our Shaman will take us on a dance …

Gate 2: The Journey of the Tarot Shaman

Our first Gated Spread told us what we must overcome to make progress and we acted upon this divination today. You will have received the reward indicated by the spread, or at least deepened your appreciation of what holds you back from progress.

So for our second Gate, we set off on our journey to prepare for our later meeting of our Animal Guide - which will follow in the week, with further teaching on Animal Symbolism.

You will need at least 10 minutes or more, your deck & a small notebook and pen/pencil – and suitable clothing for the weather conditions and environment in which you are situated, because you may be going outside!

To commence the spread, shuffle your deck considering all the journeys you have been upon. Consider what you learnt, who you saw, what you recall.

When you are ready, stop shuffling and take the top card from your deck. We do not use reversals (upside-down cards, see *Tarot Turn* for a complete guide to reversed cards) in this particular gate spread.

Make a note of the card in your notepad, and perhaps a brief note (to be expanded later) as to what it tells you about JOURNEYS.

For example, I pull the **Knight of Cups** from Roxi Sim's *Pearls of Wisdom* deck. He tells me that the Journey should always be full of delight, and not to miss the opportunity to go on detours to interesting places along the way!

You then make a journey — even if it is only into another room in the house, or outside, based on that card. For example, I chose to go down into the kitchen from the library (Cups). When you are in that new location, choose the next card, and do the same as before — in fact, I got the **Knight of Swords**, which told me I must be prepared for a journey and cut through things quickly! So I simply walked across to the drawers and picked out a small (blunt!) knife.

Continue to work through the cards, taking either small steps, going on long-distance journeys, picking items up along the way, or simply learning about journeying from the comfort of your armchair!

STOP when you reach a place or lesson from the cards that **just feels right**. If you are in any doubt, it is not the place. Make a note of the final card which you have received to have brought you to this place or taught you a particular lesson about journeying.

You may have pulled 3 cards and not moved at all, you may have pulled 30 cards and travelled a hundred miles in the day. It is up to your journey.

When you are at this place or point — begin to consider how far you have come since you started the journey. Consider what you learnt yesterday about your fears and what must be overcome. Find strength renewed in this place, which is a "power spot" as it is called in the works of Carlos Castenda, who wrote about the Yaqui Shaman, Don Juan.

When you have contemplated this journey, you can return! You may return to this spot again, or it may just be a one-off visit. You can even make a map of the cards and the locations through which you have journeyed! This is what we call a geographical spread, such as the one you can download at:

http://www.Tarotprofessionals.com/tarosophy/12Spreads.pdf

where we teach using your property as a spread!

We will then begin to summon our Animal Spirit and learn about Animal Symbolism in the cards in our next Gate exercise tomorrow. You are encouraged to share your decisions, actions and experiences on the forum, but only if you wish to do so. We have found in previous gated spreads that sharing often reveals profound similarities and interesting differences in the lives of those sharing the experience.

The Tarot Shaman III

The symbolism of Tarot is populated with animals – birds, reptiles, fish, and mammals, real and imaginary. A wonderful example of how these are used as complex symbols is the exquisitely-named but hardly-known article here:

http://www.realmagick.com/articles/39/2039.html

This article, *The Aviary at the Gates of Heaven* discusses the birds used on the Empress Tarot card in the Thoth Tarot.

However, in the Shamanic traditions, animals are seen as messengers and guides – spirits in their own right. Whilst we will examine this symbolism more tomorrow, for today we are going to do a very simple exercise to start to summon our animal guide.

The Summoning

In this next gate, having proven ourselves and embarked on a journey, we will take our sacred place and begin to summon a spirit of an animal from our Tarot deck. First we must have the animal choose us – by consulting with what the Sufis call the "Counsel".

This exercise is rather simple. Go through your deck and select out all the cards that have an animal on them. If you are using a pagan deck or animal oracle deck this may be all of the cards, of course! If your deck has no animals at all, you may wish to select an alternative deck.

Then shuffle, and place these cards FACE-DOWN about you, on the floor, in any pattern – perhaps a circle. Take any natural object, such as a crystal, stick or stone, and place it about the centre of the spread.

Begin to move the object around, feeling it respond to the cards.

When the sensation of calling or pulling is strongest, place it upon that card.

Leave the object there. DO NOT LOOK AT THE CARD. Put the other cards away.

Now spend the day wondering what the spirit of the card is – try and see its calling you or summoning in the activities of the day.

At the end of the day, you can write down your experiences and look at the card – comparing your feelings and the animal you see on the card.

The Tarot Shaman IV

Now we approach the last stages of our first experience of Tarot Shamanism, today we are going to create a special sigil – magical symbol – to focus the energy of our Animal. We are going to do this by performing a special type of one-card reading called a "drill-down" reading.

The Spirit Catcher

This Spirit Catcher is in some ways similar to a *Veve* in Voodoo traditions or a *talisman* in the Western esoteric traditions. In a sense it is also a *mandala*. It acts as a focus of the energies of the spirit. It can be used by placing it on one's personal altar, hiding it somewhere of import, or carrying it about on ones person. You may wish to take this magical diagram to the place of power you discovered in your Journey Gate and ritually burn it or bury it.

Gate 4: Creating a Spirit Catcher

Take your deck and shuffle it whilst considering the guardian you have overcome and the journey you took, and the animal which was revealed at the last gate. Concentrate on that animal and ask "How May I honor your Spirit?" Take out one card.

Lay the card face-up and make a note of the key symbols, items, objects, colors even, in each of the following areas of the card:

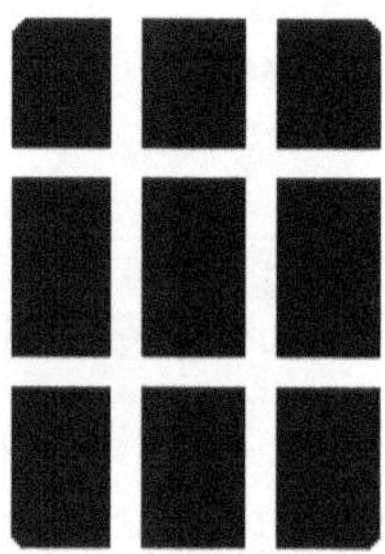

So it might be that the upper-left section of the card contains just sky. You could write in that section of the box, "Blue" or "Sky". Select the most prominent symbol in that area of the card for YOU, whilst also thinking of the animal.

Then imagine that this box represents a new Spread.

The top two sections are "How you Honor me in your spiritual life", the middle two sections are "How you Honor me in your thoughts and feelings" and the bottom two sections are "How you Honor me in your daily activities". These are the three levels of the world.

Take each of the two symbols and read them as if they were a pair of very simple Tarot or Oracle cards. What comes to mind? Write down your feelings and impressions.

In this manner of reading, each individual card becomes a *Mandala*. It is also a spirit catcher in that for the next two days you must live according to these divinations before completing the last Gate. These activities must honour your ANIMAL SPIRIT in all levels of your life. You should also record any dreams or events of note during this time.

You are encouraged to share your discoveries in the forum.

The Tarot Shaman V

We come now to the final Gate of this week-long Gated Spreads experience. We hope you have enjoyed learning about the Tarot through the animal symbolism of the cards and by engaging with your life in a Shamanistic approach. We have also looked at the concept of "drill-down" reading with one-card spreads.

In this final Gate we pull together our experience by embodying and being empowered by the animal spirit we have been called by and which we have caught by honoring it.

The Invocation of the Animal Spirit

We now invoke and embody the Animal Spirit. This step uses a variation of a magical practice taught by urban shaman and modern chaos magician Jan Fries, whose books we recommend, particularly *Visual Magick*.

Living the Animal

On a largish sheet of paper, draw a rough sketch of your Animal Spirit. This can be heavily stylistic, symbolic or realistic.

Place a cross on 5 places on your picture. These could be key features such as the eye, a wing, tail, etc. Write in each position, "This is the vision of my spirit", "This is the spiritual power of my spirit", "This is the balance of my spirit" or whatever may be appropriate to that part of the animal.

Now take your deck and shuffle whilst contemplating the journey that has brought you to this place, the fear you had to overcome, the calling and the catching, and the honoring of your animal spirit.

All the Gates have led to this divine moment.

Take out a card when you are ready for each of the place on the animal. These cards represent the animal's response to you. They are the divination for how you can invoke these powers and qualities of your animal spirit. They tell you how to live the animal.

So for example, if I had a bat, and I had placed one of my crosses on its ear(s), writing, "This is the secret sense of the Bat, my spirit", and then drawn the 7 of Disks (Thoth Tarot) in that position, I would read it as follows: "Failure and Sloth – the secret sense of my animal spirit is present and invoked when I give up trying and relax, surrender."

You will now have five points of invocation of your Animal Spirit. As a Tarot Shaman you can use these cards to draw upon the power of your animal guide, perhaps leaving them visible in your sight before sleep and communing with your animal in dreams.

You may also create a montage of the cards chosen to represent your animal, or otherwise use the cards to remind you of all that you have learnt during this week.

There are many other shamanistic methods of exploring the Tarot, and many aspects of animal symbolism which can be pursued. We trust this week has given you a new angle on your Tarot, and look forward to welcoming you on other Gated Spreads in the future.

Please do feel free to continue discussion in the Tarot-Town.com forum for this experience! And remember that all change is done in our own workshop.

> When a Navajo person wishes to renew or re-establish, in the world, the harmonious condition of well being and beauty expressed by the Navajo word 'hozho' he must first strive, through ritual, to create this harmony and peacefulness within his own being. Having established such 'hozho' within himself, he can that actively impart this state of well-being to the enveloping cosmos, through the transforming power of song or prayer, finally, according to Witherspoon.

After a person has projected 'hozho' into the air through ritual form, he then, at the conclusion of the ritual, breathes that 'hozho' back into himself and makes himself a part of the order, harmony, and beauty he has projected into the world through the ritual of speech and song.

The Spell of the Sensuous (p. 236)

I grew up with packet transmission, as did anyone reading this in 2012 who is in their 40's. The impact of this concept, an electronic protocol designed to run on anything from "two cans and a piece of string" hardly needs stating. The mysterious method of ensuring a communication reaches its destination, and is confirmed as doing so, no matter what links in the connecting chain are broken – routing – is a de facto element of modern society. This TCP/IP protocol is the bedrock concept of the internet and all that operates upon that platform.

In 1988, IRC (Internet Relay Chat) was launched and just two years later Tim Berners-Lee created "the internet", actually the http protocol linking "pages" together which sat on TCP/IP and in effect gave a larger audience a reason for viewing and connecting to the previous green-screen code.

In that same year, a group of Tarot authors, teachers and artists gathered in Los Angeles for the First International Newcastle Tarot Symposium, whose presentations are recorded in *New Thoughts in Tarot: A Symposium Journal*, ed. Mary K. Greer and Rachel Pollack. One of these was the late Nicholas Tereschenko (1916 - 2002), whose presentation was entitled 'Arcanum XXIII: The Drowned Sleeping Titan', upon the Hanged Man card.

In a neat synchronicity, I (Marcus) met Nick at the Golden Dawn Centenary Conference in London, 1987, and discussed this subject – which was to later be of great relevance to the Waite-Trinick Tarot project some 22 years later. I was, of course, 22 at the time – perhaps that number has some significance.

Tereschenko, a gifted teacher of esoteric traditions, and in particular the Gurdjieffian Fourth Way work, developed the existing term, *Hapax Legomena*, to refer to a word only used once in a written language. He produced a glossary of over 500 such words from the work of Gurdjieff.

One such neologism – new word – is *being-Partkdolg-duty*, which refers to the work of conscious labor and intentional suffering. It is this "partkdolg" that brings about transformation, through self-observation, self-remembering, active mentation and contemplation. This latter can also be translated as the more whimsical "pondering". These practices generate what Gurdjieff called *Zernofookalnian-friction*, leading to new perception.

It occurs to us also that every Tarot reading is a *Hapax Legomena*, a unique statement or "word". In the new world of amusement, instant gratification, and lack of connection, we should aim to write a *Hapax* with every reading – recognize that in that moment of divination, a divine moment is present.

In the Last Light of the World

> There is not enough darkness in all the world to put out the light of even one small candle.

> *Robert Alden*

As we have seen, the Tens of the Minors symbolize, Kabbalistically and numerologically, the very last descent of spirit into matter. We began this book with the Fool, and now we conclude with the Tens.

The Tens, according to Crowley, are the "end of all energy" *(Book of Thoth,* p. 187). They represent:

Pentacles:	Wealth
Swords:	Ruin
Cups:	Satiety
Wands:	Oppression

In each of these is the final extension of their Ace, the roots now grown of our cosmic tree, upside-down from the heavens. In our daily life, we seek wealth, yet there is nothing more we can do with it than spend; we fight, and all ends in violence; we crave, and our cravings are their own despair; we seek empowerment, and bring about tyranny. There is no escape from the Black Iron Prison, unless we transcend it totally and utterly. We are always one foolish step from freedom, and that step is here and now.

We leave this book with a thought about inspiration. As John Fowles wrote in his lesser-known book, but highly recommended, *The Aristos*, a collection of several hundred paragraph statements of his beliefs, "this book was first published against the advice of almost everyone who read it". He went on to explain that rather than his damaging any reputation, it was "not just the matter of the book that offended. It was the manner as well – the dogmatic way in which I set out my views on life. But that too sprang from a desire to nourish individuality. By stating baldly what *I* believe I hope to force you to state baldly to yourself what *you* believe. I do not expect agreement." (*The Aristos*, pp. 7-8).

We hope this book has inspired you to consider your own thoughts on Tarot, beyond the box. And it does seem fitting to complete this present work with those words, from the author of *The Magus*.

Marcus Katz & Tali Goodwin
Keswick, February 2012.

> The closer you come to the end. The more there is to say. The end is only imaginary, a destination you invent to keep yourself going.
>
> *The Country of Last Things* (p. 183)

The **Tyldwick Tarot**, whose images grace the covers of this Tarosophy Kickstart series, is a fully complete Tarot deck awaiting publishing by Neil Lovell. It can be viewed online on the comprehensive and beautifully designed site:

http://www.malpertuis.co.uk/tyldwick

The theme of the deck is that of an elegant house, through which one can wander without "being distracted by a cast of characters" as might be found in other Tarot decks. The cards are beautifully layered and suffused with tonal casts from the international travel that the designer has enjoyed – and not so enjoyed - as described in some fascinating cases which are revealed in the extensive interview on the site.

The deck reminds us very much of the film, *Last Year in Marienbad* (1961, dir. Alain Resnais) which is a dream-like excursion into an environment which may or may not be real, in which the characters not so much inhabit the place, but are extensions of the place itself. In the Tyldwick Tarot, the few characters we see are the Court Cards where faces are reflected in mirrors – or perhaps are even looking out from the other side of the mirrors themselves.

We would highly recommend this deck, and suggest you make that commitment – as we would love to see it in our own hands and use it for both reading and meditation work.

Conclusion

We trust you will find many months of discovery and play with your decks in this third Tarosophy KickStart Guide. It has been a pleasure to produce it and play with the ideas to provide a fresh new look at Tarot.

It is hoped you will feel inspired to play with your deck as a living and breathing oracle in engagement with the world around you. Our second volume of Kickstart Guides commences with *TAROT SWITCH,* which explores how to use Tarot in engaging change in your everyday life.

These Guides are a prompt for your own exploration, to discover your own voice in Tarot. We encourage the diversity of divination!

We have also provided in the final section a list of reading materials and website resources to discover more in the very best of Tarot and Tarosophy®.

Titles in this innovative series of Tarosophy® KickStart Guides.

Volume I.

Book I: *Tarot Flip* - Reading Tarot Straight from the Box
Book II: *Tarot Twist* - Finding a Spread for Every Question
Book III: *Tarot Inspire* – Explore your Spiritual Life with Tarot

Volume II.

Book I: *Tarot Switch* – Use Magical Tarot methods to change your Life
Book II: *Tarot Uplift* – Experience Tarot and Kabbalah for Initiation
Book III: *Tarot Divine* - Encounter the Mystical Teachings of Tarot

Bibliography

Abram, David. *The Spell of the Sensuous*. New York: Vintage Press, 1996.

Anonymous, *Meditations on the Tarot*. Rockport: Element Books Ltd, 1991.

Auger, Emily E. (ed.), *Tarot in Culture*, Australia: ATS, forthcoming.

Auster, Paul. *In the Country of Last Things*. New York: Faber and Faber Ltd, 1987.

Bennett, J.G. *A Spiritual Psychology*. Sherborne: Coome Springs Press, 1974.

Crowley, Aleister, *The Book of Thoth*. York Beach: Samuel Weiser, 1985.

Da Love Ananda, *The Love-Ananda Gita*, Clearlake: Dawn Horse Press, 1989.

Echols, S.E., Mueller, R. & Thomson, S.A. *Spiritual Tarot*. New York: Avon Books, 1996.

Eco, Umberto, *Foucault's Pendulum*, London: Picador, 1990.

Eco, Umberto, *In the Name of the Rose*. London: Pan Books Ltd, 1984.

Edward Beck, Don and Cowan. C. Christopher. S. *Spiral Dynamics*. Oxford: Blackwell 2003.

Fienstein, D & Krippner, S. *Personal Mythology: The Psychology of your Evolving Self*. Tarcher, 1988.

Flower, Michael Attyah. *The Seer in Ancient Greece*, Berkley and Los Angeles: California Press, 2009.

Fowles, John. *The Aristos*. London: Pan Books, 1968.

Free John, Da. *The Four Fundamental Questions*. Clear Lake Highlands: The Dawn Hall Press, 1980.

Gilbert, Tony. *Messages From the Archetypes*. Ashland: Whiteland Press, 2004.

Godden, Rumer, *Diddakoi*, Macmillians Children's Press.

Gold, E.J. *Life in the Labyrinth*. Nevada City: IDHHB, Inc, 1986.

Gold, E.J. *The Human Biological Machine as a Transformational Apparatus*. Nevada City: IDDHHB, 1985.

Greer, M.K, Pollack, Rachel. *New Thoughts on Tarot, Symposium Journal*. North Hollywood: New Castle Publishing., Co Inc, 1989.

Grey, Eden. *Mastering the Tarot*. New York: Crown Press, 1971.

Hall, James A. *Jungian Dream Interpretation*. Toronto: Inner City Books, 1983.

Hamaker-Zondag, Karen. *Tarot as a Way of Life*. York Beach: Weiser, 1997.

Haule, R. *Pilgrimage of the Heart: The Path of Romantic Love*. Boston: Shambahala Publications, Inc, 1992.

Hillman, James and Ventura, Michael. *We've had a Hundred Years of Psychotherapy and the World's Getting Worse*. New York: Harper Collins, 1993.

Hoeller, Stephen. *The Fools Pilgrimage*. Wheaton: The Theosophical Publishing House, 2004.

Holman, John. *The Return of the Perennial Philosophy*. London: Watkins Publishing, 2008.

Hutton, Alice. *The Cards Can't Lie*. London: Jupiter Books, 1979.

Huxley, Aldous. *The Perennial Philosophy*. New York: Harper Collins, 2009.

Iles Johnson, Sarah. *Ancient Greek Divination*. Chichester: Wiley-Blackwell, 2008.

Jodorowsky, Alejandro, *The Way of the Tarot*. Rochester: Destiny Books, 2009.

Kaplan, Stuart R., *The Encyclopedia of Tarot Vol I*. New York: US Games Systems, 1985.

Katz, Marcus, *Tarosophy*, Keswick: Forge Press, 2016.

Kelper, Thomas, S. *Mystical Writings of Rulman Merswin*. Philadelphia: The Westminster Press, n.d.

Lehrer, Johnah. *How We Decide*. New York: First Mariner Press, 2010.

Leon, Dai, *Origins of the Tarot*. Berkeley: Frog Books, 2009.

Mathers, MacGregor S.L. *The Kabbalah Unveiled*. Trowbridge: Routledge & Kegan Paul, 1981.

Markus Montola, Jaakko Stenros, Annika Waern, *Pervasive Games: Theory and Design*, Oxford: Elsevier, 2009.

Nichols, Sallie. *Jung: An Archetypal Journey*. York Beach: Weiser, 1984.

Nouwen, J. M. *The Inner Voice of Love*. London: Darton, Longman and Todd Ltd, 1997.

Nouwen, J.M. *The Wounded Healer*. New York: Darton, Longman and Todd Ltd, 1994.

Ouspensky, P.D. *Tertium Organum.* London: Routledge& Keegan, 1981.

Ozaniec, Naomi. *The Element Tarot Handbook.* Shaftsbury: Element Books Ltd, 1994.

Parish, Bobbi L. Parish. New York. *Create Your Personal Sacred Text.* Broadway Books, 1999.

Peake, Anthony. *The Daemon: A Guide To Your Extraordinary Secret Self.* London: Arcturus, 2008.

Pollack, Rachel. *The Forest of Souls.* St. Paul: Llewellyn, 2003.

Roberts, Bernadette, *The Path to No Self,* Boston: Shamballa, 1985.

Sandford, Linda, T. *Strong at the Broken Places.* London: Virago Press, 1991.

Schroer, Silvia, Staubli, Thomas, Maloney, Linda. *Body Symbolism in the Bible,* Wilmington: Michael Glazier, 2001.

Sedgwick, David. *The Wounded Healer.* New York: Routledge, 2009.

Sterling, Steven Walter. *Tarot Awareness: Exploring the Spiritual Path.* Minnesota: Llewellyn Worldwide, 2000.

Sturgess, Russell. *Metanoia: Renovating the House of your Spirit.* Queensland: beAttitude, 2009.

Templar, Eldon. *The Path of the Magus.* Kettering: Mark Saunders Books, 1986.

Tennov, Dorothy. *Love & Limerence: The Experience of Being in Love.* New York: Stein and Day Publishers, 1980.

Tweedy, Irina, *Daughter of Fire.* Nevada City: Blue Dolphin, 1986.

Underhill, Evelyn, *Mysticism: A Study in the Nature and Development of Man's Spiritual Consciousness*. London: Methuen & Co, 1942.

Vandenberg, Phillip. *Mysteries of the Oracles*. London: TPP, 2007.

Wallace,I. Mark. *Finding God in the Singing River*. Minneapolis: Fortress Press, 1971.

Wilson, Robert Anton. *Coincidance*. Phoenix: Falcon Press, 1988.

Zaidman, Louise Bruit & Schmitt Pantel, Pauline. *Religion in the Ancient Greek City*. Newcastle-Upon-Tyne; Cambridge Press, 1994.

Websites & Resources

Tarot Association: http://www.tarotprofessionals.com

Tarot Professionals Facebook Group

http://www.facebook.com/groups/tarotprofessionals

Free Tarot Card Meanings & Spreads

http://www.mytarotcardmeanings.com